Jeremy Walenn

English for
LAW
in Higher Education Studies

Course Book

Series editor: Terry Phillips

English for Specific Academic Purposes

Garnet
EDUCATION

Published by
Garnet Publishing Ltd.
8 Southern Court
South Street
Reading RG1 4QS, UK

First published 2009
Reprinted 2009.

ISBN 978 1 85964 417 1

British Cataloguing-in-Publication Data
A catalogue record for this book is available from
the British Library.

Production
Series editor: Terry Phillips
Lead authors: Carolyn Walker, Marian Dunn
Project management: Martin Moore, Bruce Nicholson
Editorial team: Louise Elkins, Charlotte Abberley
Academic review: Professor Rosemary Auchmuty, University
of Reading; James Lee, Birmingham Law School, University
of Birmingham
Design: Henry Design Associates and Mike Hinks
Photography: Sally Henry and Trevor Cook; Alamy (Jenny
Matthews); Bettmann; Bongarts; Corbis; Clipart.com; face
to face Bildagentur; Getty Images (Matt Cardy, Jonathan
Daniel, Graeme Robertson); Hulton-Deutsch Collection;
Image Source; Photofusion Picture Library; Photostock

Audio recorded at Motivation Sound Studios produced by
EFS Television Production Ltd.

The author and publisher would like to thank Google for
permission to reproduce the results listings on page 35; Don
S. Browning, *The United Nations Convention on the Rights
of the Child: Should It Be Ratified and Why?*, 20 Emory Int'l
L. Rev. 157 (2006) for permission to reproduce part of this
article on page 97; CIEL (the Center for International
Environmental Law) for permission to adapt material from
their website on page 91.

Every effort has been made to trace copyright holders and
we apologize in advance for any unintentional omission. We
will be happy to insert the appropriate acknowledgements
in any subsequent editions.

Printed and bound in Lebanon by International Press

Introduction

English for Law is designed for students who plan to take a law course entirely or partly in English. The principal aim of *English for Law* is to teach students to cope with input texts, i.e., listening and reading, in the discipline. However, students will be expected to produce output texts in speech and writing throughout the course.

The syllabus focuses on key vocabulary for the discipline and on words and phrases commonly used in academic English. It covers key facts and concepts from the discipline, thereby giving students a flying start for when they meet the same points again in their faculty work. It also focuses on the skills that will enable students to get the most out of lectures and written texts. Finally, it presents the skills required to take part in seminars and tutorials and to produce essay assignments.

English for Law comprises:

- student Course Book including audio transcripts and wordlist
- the Teacher's Book, which provides detailed guidance on each lesson, full answer keys, audio transcripts and extra photocopiable resources
- audio CDs with lecture and seminar excerpts

English for Law has 12 units, each of which is based on a different aspect of law. Odd-numbered units are based on listening (lecture/seminar extracts). Even-numbered units are based on reading.

Each unit is divided into four lessons:

Lesson 1: vocabulary for the discipline; vocabulary skills such as word-building, use of affixes, use of synonyms for paraphrasing

Lesson 2: reading or listening text and skills development

Lesson 3: reading or listening skills extension. In addition, in later reading units, students are introduced to a writing assignment which is further developed in Lesson 4; in later listening units, students are introduced to a spoken language point (e.g., making an oral presentation at a seminar) which is further developed in Lesson 4

Lesson 4: a parallel listening or reading text to that presented in Lesson 2 which students have to use their new skills (Lesson 3) to decode; in addition, written or spoken work is further practised

The last two pages of each unit, *Vocabulary bank* and *Skills bank*, are a useful summary of the unit content.

Each unit provides between 4 and 6 hours of classroom activity with the possibility of a further 2-4 hours on the suggested extra activities. The course will be suitable, therefore, as the core component of a faculty-specific pre-sessional or foundation course of between 50 and 80 hours.

It is assumed that prior to using this book students will already have completed a general EAP (English for Academic Purposes) course such as *Skills in English* (Garnet Publishing, up to the end at least of Level 3), and will have achieved an IELTS level of at least 5.

For a list of other titles in this series, see www.garneteducation.com/

Book map

Unit	Topics
1 Law and order Listening · Speaking	• branches of law • key features of law
2 Landmarks in law Reading · Writing	• historical landmarks in the development of law • Lord Denning and 20th century English law • judicial precedent
3 Crimes and civil wrongs Listening · Speaking	• tort v crime • criminal and civil courts • trespass to the person
4 Computers in law Reading · Writing	• computers for research • types of legal information available on the web
5 Theft 1: the Theft Act Listening · Speaking	• definition of theft • components of theft • important case law
6 Theft 2: appropriation Reading · Writing	• taking without owner's consent • differences between: burglary, aggravated burglary and robbery
7 Contract law 1: consideration Listening · Speaking	• definition of a contract • doctrine of consideration • judicial interpretation
8 Contract law 2: misrepresentation Reading · Writing	• four types of misrepresentation: fraudulent misrepresentation · negligent misrepresentation · wholly innocent misrepresentation · negligent misrepresentation under statute
9 Employment law Listening · Speaking	• fair, unfair and wrongful dismissal • employment tribunals
10 Homicide Reading · Writing	• types of homicide • defences to homicide • murder v manslaughter
11 International law Listening · Speaking	• origins of international law • influence of international law on domestic law • international law and the environment
12 Human rights law Reading · Writing	• UN Charter of Human Rights • UN Convention on the Rights of the Child • equal opportunities

Vocabulary focus	Skills focus		Unit
• words from general English with a special meaning in law • prefixes and suffixes	**Listening**	• preparing for a lecture • predicting lecture content from the introduction • understanding lecture organization • choosing an appropriate form of notes • making lecture notes	**1**
	Speaking	• speaking from notes	
• English–English dictionaries: headwords · definitions · parts of speech · phonemes · stress markers · countable/uncountable · transitive/intransitive	**Reading**	• using research questions to focus on relevant information in a text • using topic sentences to get an overview of the text	**2**
	Writing	• writing topic sentences • summarizing a text	
• stress patterns in multi-syllable words • prefixes	**Listening**	• preparing for a lecture • predicting lecture content • making lecture notes • using different information sources	**3**
	Speaking	• reporting research findings • formulating questions	
• computer jargon • abbreviations and acronyms • discourse and stance markers • verb and noun suffixes	**Reading**	• identifying topic development within a paragraph • using the Internet effectively • evaluating Internet search results	**4**
	Writing	• reporting research findings	
• word sets: synonyms, antonyms, etc. • common lecture language	**Listening**	• understanding 'signpost language' in lectures • using symbols and abbreviations in note-taking	**5**
	Speaking	• making effective contributions to a seminar	
• synonyms, replacement subjects, etc. for sentence-level paraphrasing	**Reading**	• locating key information in complex sentences	**6**
	Writing	• reporting findings from other sources: paraphrasing • writing complex sentences	
• compound nouns • fixed phrases from legal English • fixed phrases from academic English • common lecture language	**Listening**	• understanding speaker emphasis	**7**
	Speaking	• asking for clarification • responding to queries and requests for clarification	
• synonyms • nouns from verbs • definitions • common 'direction' verbs in essay titles (*discuss*, *analyse*, *evaluate*, etc.)	**Reading**	• understanding dependent clauses with passives	**8**
	Writing	• paraphrasing • expanding notes into complex sentences • recognizing different essay types/structures: descriptive · analytical · comparison/evaluation ·argument • writing essay plans • writing essays	
• fixed phrases from legal English • fixed phrases from academic English	**Listening**	• using the Cornell note-taking system • recognizing digressions in lectures	**9**
	Speaking	• making effective contributions to a seminar • referring to other people's ideas in a seminar	
• 'neutral' and 'marked' words • fixed phrases from legal English • fixed phrases from academic English	**Reading**	• recognizing the writer's stance and level of confidence or tentativeness • inferring implicit ideas	**10**
	Writing	• writing essays • using direct quotations • compiling a bibliography/reference list	
• words/phrases used to link ideas (*moreover*, *as a result*, etc.) • stress patterns in noun phrases and compounds • fixed phrases from academic English	**Listening**	• recognizing the speaker's stance • writing up notes in full	**11**
	Speaking	• building an argument in a seminar • agreeing/disagreeing	
• verbs used to introduce ideas from other sources (*X contends/suggests/asserts that* …) • linking words/phrases conveying contrast (*whereas*), result (*consequently*), reasons (*due to*), etc. • words for quantities (*a significant minority*)	**Reading**	• understanding how ideas in a text are linked	**12**
	Writing	• deciding whether to use direct quotation or paraphrase • incorporating quotations • writing research reports • writing effective introductions/conclusions	

1 LAW AND ORDER

1.1 Vocabulary   guessing words in context • prefixes and suffixes

A Read the text. The red words are probably familiar to you in general English. But can you think of a different meaning for each word in legal English?

> My friend walked into the bar. He was carrying a small case. We had a brief conversation about the weather and then started chatting about last night's football match. I had hardly finished a sentence when he complained that his team had lost because the defence had been really bad. They had played without any conviction. I took a stand against him and said you shouldn't judge a team on the evidence of just one match.

B Read these sentences from legal texts. Complete each sentence with one of the red words from Exercise A.

1 The ＿＿＿＿＿＿＿＿ asked the members of the jury to leave the court.

2 A solicitor gives a ＿＿＿＿＿＿＿＿ to the barrister which consists of important legal documents.

3 My lawyer disagreed with the verdict and wants my ＿＿＿＿＿＿＿＿ to go to a higher court.

4 The accused was shocked when he was found guilty and given a four-year prison ＿＿＿＿＿＿＿＿ .

5 I think she already has a ＿＿＿＿＿＿＿＿ for shoplifting.

6 As the key witness took the ＿＿＿＿＿＿＿＿ there was complete silence in the court.

7 The prosecution hasn't got enough ＿＿＿＿＿＿＿＿ to secure a guilty verdict.

8 Barristers are lawyers who have been called to the ＿＿＿＿＿＿＿＿ .

9 The lawyers for the ＿＿＿＿＿＿＿＿ complained that their client could not get a fair trial.

C Study the words in box a.
1 What is the connection between all the words?
2 What is the base word in each case?
3 What do we call the extra letters?
4 What is the meaning of each prefix?
5 Can you think of another word with each prefix?

> **a** dishonest   enforce   illegal
> impartial   indecisive
> international   jurisdiction
> mistrial   unjust

D Study the words in box b.
1 What is the connection between all the words?
2 What is the base word in each case?
3 What do we call the extra letters?
4 What effect do the extra letters have on the base word?
5 Can you think of another word with each suffix?

> **b**   acceptable   accusation
> adversarial   defendant
> inquisitorial   judgment   justice
> prosecution   solicitor   statutory

E Discuss the picture on the opposite page using words from this page.

A You are a student in the Law Faculty of Hadford University. The title of your first lecture is *What is law?*

  1 Write a definition of law.

  2 What other ideas will be in this lecture? Make some notes.

See Skills bank

B 🎧 Listen to Part 1 of the talk. What does the lecturer say about law? Tick one or more of the following.

  a It is about rules. _____

  b It is about not doing things. _____

  c It is about punishment. _____

  d It is more complex than this. _____

C In Part 2 of the talk, the lecturer mentions *bar, fair* and *just.*

  1 What do these words mean in general English?

  2 What do they mean in law?

  3 🎧 Listen and check your ideas.

D In Part 3 of the talk, the lecturer describes different branches or types of law.

  1 How many branches or types can you think of?

  2 🎧 Listen and check your ideas.

  3 What aspect of law does the lecturer think is now very important?

E 🎧 In the final part of the talk, the lecturer gives a definition of law and some examples. Listen and mark each word in the box **D** if it is part of the definition and **E** if it is part of the example.

> set _____   rules _____   drive _____
>
> forbid _____   speed _____   require _____
>
> limit _____   camera _____   actions _____

F Write a definition of law. Use words from Exercise E.

G Look back at your notes from Exercise A. Did you predict:

- the main ideas?
- most of the special vocabulary?
- the order of information?

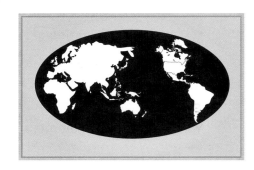

1.3 Extending skills

lecture organization • choosing the best form of notes

A In a court, who can ...

1 pass a sentence?

2 reach a verdict?

3 defend the accused?

4 give evidence?

5 take down the transcript?

6 be found guilty?

B How can you organize information in a lecture? Match the beginnings and endings.

1 question and

2 problem and

3 classification and

4 advantages and

5 comparison and

6 cause and

7 sequence of

8 stages of a

9 theories or opinions then

contrast

definition

disadvantages

effect

events

supporting information

process

solution

answer

C How can you record information during a lecture? Match the illustrations to the words and phrases in the box.

tree diagram   flowchart   headings and notes   spidergram   table   timeline   two columns

D Match each organization of information in Exercise B with a method of note-taking from Exercise C. You can use one method for different types of organization.

E 🎧 Listen to five lecture introductions. Choose a possible way to take notes from Exercise C in each case.

Example:

You hear: *OK, good morning, everyone. Today we're going to look at the way the court system in England and Wales is organized ...*

You choose: *tree diagram*

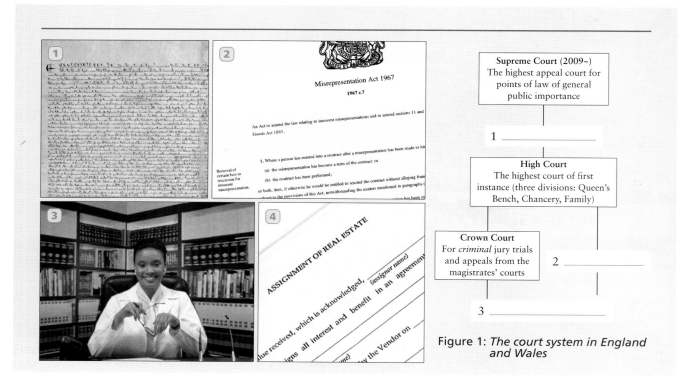

Figure 1: *The court system in England and Wales*

A Say these pairs of words from this unit. What are the main changes in pronunciation?

  1 law/lawyer   **4** bar/barrister

  2 jury/juror   **5** crime/criminal

  3 break/breach

B Look at the pictures and diagram above.

  1 Name the items in pictures 1–4. Use words from the box.

> statute   Magna Carta   contract   solicitor's office

  2 Complete the diagram of the court system in England and Wales in Figure 1.

C 🎧 Cover the opposite page. Listen to the lecture introductions from Lesson 3 again. Make an outline on a separate sheet of paper for each introduction.

D Look at your outline for each lecture. What do you expect the lecturer to talk about in the lecture? In what order?

E 🎧 Listen to the next part of each lecture. Complete your notes.

F Uncover the opposite page. Check your notes with the model notes. Are yours the same or different?

G Work in pairs.

  1 Use the notes on the opposite page. Reconstruct one lecture.

  2 Give the lecture to another pair.

①

Supreme Court
(civ. + crim.)

|

Court of Appeal
(civ. div. + crim. div.)

|

High Court
(Queen's Bench, Chancery, Fam. div.)

County Court   Crown Court
(civ.)   (crim.)

magistrates' court

②

The jury system

+	−
ensures a fair trial esp. in criminal cases	some cases too complex for ordinary people, e.g., serious fraud
people from a wide spectrum of society	too many unemployed/retired people
decide only on facts of case	swayed by emotion

③

Statutory interpretation

(how courts understand laws passed by Parl.)

1) literal rule (ordinary meaning in dictionary)

2) mischief rule (to address the wrong)

3) golden rule (meaning that best fits situation)

④

Dev. of statutory + common law
in English legal system

1066 William the Conqueror defeated Harold at Battle of Hastings

↓

1154 Henry II created unified system of law + court system

↓

1189 'Time immemorial' – introduction of common law system

↓

1204 King John lost lands in France → higher taxes → barons angry

↓

1215 King John forced to sign Magna Carta
no imprisonment without trial

⑤

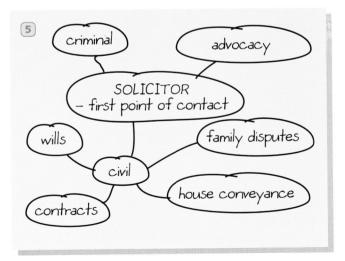

criminal — advocacy

SOLICITOR
– first point of contact

wills — civil — family disputes

contracts — house conveyance

Guessing words in context

Using related words

Sometimes a word in general English has a special meaning in law.

Examples:
bar, sentence, defence, just, brief, case

If you recognize a word but don't understand it in context, think:
What is the basic meaning of the word? Does that help me understand the special meaning?

Example:
*A **bar** is a barrier that someone stands behind in order to take orders from customers. So, the **bar** is the place that a barrister stands behind in order to deliver a speech.*

Removing prefixes

A **prefix** = letters at the **start of a word**.

A prefix changes the meaning of a word.

Examples:
redo – do again
miscalculate – calculate wrongly

If you don't recognize a word, think: *Is there a prefix?* Remove it. Do you recognize the word now? What does that prefix mean? Add it to the meaning of the word.

Removing suffixes

A **suffix** = letters at the **end of a word.**

A suffix sometimes changes the **part of speech** of the word.

Examples:
accuse ➔ *accusation* = verb ➔ noun
decide ➔ *decisive* = verb ➔ adjective

A suffix sometimes changes the meaning **in a predictable way.**

Examples:
pressure + ize (or *ise*) – make into:
The police pressurized the accused into making a confession.

weak + en – make or make more:
The evidence from the eye witness weakened the defence.

rely + able – able to (be relied on):
She is a reliable authority on handwriting.

If you don't recognize a word, think: *Is there a suffix?* Remove it. Do you recognize the word now? What does that suffix mean? Add it to the meaning of the word.

Making the most of lectures

Before a lecture ...

Plan
- Find out the topic of the lecture.
- Research the topic.
- Check the pronunciation of names and key words in English.

Prepare
- Get to the lecture room early.
- Sit where you can see and hear clearly.
- Bring any equipment you may need.
- Write the date, topic and name of the lecturer at the top of a sheet of paper.

During a lecture ...

Predict
- Listen carefully to the introduction. Think: *What kind of lecture is this?*
- Write an outline. Leave space for notes.
- Think of possible answers/solutions/effects, etc., while the lecturer is speaking.

Produce
- Write notes/copy from the board.
- Record sources – books/websites/names.
- At the end, ask the lecturer/other students for missing information.

Making perfect lecture notes

Choose the best way to record information from a lecture.

advantages and disadvantages	➔ two-column table
cause and effect	➔ spidergram
classification and definition	➔ tree diagram/spidergram
comparison and contrast	➔ table
facts and figures	➔ table
sequence	➔ timeline
stages of a process	➔ flowchart
question and answer	➔ headings and notes

Speaking from notes

Sometimes you have to give a short talk in a seminar on research you have done.
- Prepare the listeners with an introduction.
- Match the introduction to the type of information/notes.

2 LANDMARKS IN LAW

2.1 Vocabulary · using an English–English dictionary

A How can an English–English dictionary help you understand and produce spoken and written English?

B Study the dictionary extract on the opposite page.

1 Why are the two words (top left and top right) important?
2 How many meanings does *judicial* have? What about *judicious*?
3 Why does the word *judge* appear twice in **bold**?
4 What do we call someone who sits in a magistrates' court?
5 Where is the main stress on *judiciary*? What about *justice*?
6 What is the pronunciation of *j* in each bold word in this extract?
7 What is the pronunciation of *u* in each bold word in this extract?
8 What part of speech is *judgemental*?
9 Can we write: *The court justiced the criminal.* Why (not)?

C Look at the bold words in the dictionary extract on the opposite page.

1 What order are they in?
2 Write the words in box a in the same order.

> **a**
> case   precedent   bind   right   duty
> overturn   condition   follow
> promise   consideration   device   appeal
> persuasive   plaintiff

D Look at the top of this double page from an English–English dictionary.

1 Which word from Exercise C will appear on this page?
2 Think of words before and after some of the words in Exercise C.

> principle   prosecution

E Look up the red words in box a.

1 How many meanings can you find for each word?
2 What kind of noun/verb is each word?
3 Which meaning is most likely in legal text?

F Look up the green words in box a.

1 Where is the main stress in each word?
2 What is the sound of the underlined letter(s) in each word?
3 Which meaning is most likely in legal text?

G Test each other on the words from Exercises E and F. Give the dictionary definition of one of the words. Can your partner guess which word you are defining?

H What does the picture on the opposite page show? Use some of the words from this lesson.

judge

judge /dʒʌdʒ/ *v* [I or T] 1. to form or express an opinion about something especially after careful thought 2. to sit in judgment on something or someone in a court 3. to decide the result of a competition

judge /dʒʌdʒ/ *n* [C] 1. a lawyer who has been given the power to decide on questions brought before a court 2. a person who has been appointed to decide the winner of a competition such as ice skating

judgement /'dʒʌdʒmənt/ *n* [C] the ability to make a wise decision based on careful thought

judgment /'dʒʌdʒmənt/ *n* [C] a formal decision made by a court or a judge

judgmental or **judgemental** /dʒʌdʒ'ment(ə)l/ *adj* forming an opinion about something or someone based on morality

judicature /'dʒuːdɪkətʃə(r)/ *n* [U] the administration of the justice system

judicial /dʒuː'dɪʃ(ə)l/ *adj* matters ordered by a court or a judge: *judicial precedent*

Justice of the Peace

judiciary /dʒuː'dɪʃɪəri/ *n* [C] *pl judiciaries* the branch of government that deals with justice and forms part of the separation of powers: *the executive, the administration, the judiciary*

judicious /dʒuː'dɪʃəs/ *adj* 1. using good judgement to reach a decision 2. describing a person who shows good judgement: *The President is judicious and well respected.*

jurist /'dʒʊərɪst/ *n* [C] a person who has a deep knowledge or understanding of legal matters

juror /'dʒʊərə(r)/ *n* [C] a person who sits on a jury

jury /'dʒʊəri/ *n* [C] *pl juries* a group of people (usually twelve) chosen from the general public who sit in court to reach a decision based on the evidence they have heard

justice /'dʒʌstɪs/ *n* [U] the quality of being impartial and fair

Justice of the Peace *n* [C] *pl Justices of the Peace* a non-lawyer given the power to hear minor cases in a magistrates' court

A Name some people who have had a great influence on the development of the law.

B Study the list on the right.

1 Identify each person's achievements.

2 Describe what effect these achievements have had on the development of the law.

3 Decide which person in this list has had the greatest influence on the law.

C You are going to read a text. What should you do before you read a text in detail? See *Skills bank*

D This text is about Lord Denning, one of the most influential judges in UK law in the 20th century.

1 Think of some research questions before you read.

2 Compare your questions with those in the Hadford University assignment at the bottom of this page.

E Study these topic sentences from the text.

The Law's Hall of Fame

- Alfred the Great
- Sir William Blackstone
- Napoleon Bonaparte
- Cicero
- Sir Edward Coke
- Clarence Darrow
- Lord Denning
- Draco
- Thomas Jefferson
- Justinian

source: www.duhaime.org

(a) Alfred Thompson, Lord Denning was one of the greatest judges working in the English legal system during the 20th century.

(b) Denning also made some controversial judgments that some jurists believe damaged his reputation.

(c) As Master of the Rolls, the most senior judge in the Civil Division of the Court of Appeal, Denning challenged the principle of *stare decisis* (judicial binding precedent).

(d) In *Central London Property Trust Ltd* v *High Trees House Ltd* [1947] KB 130 Denning appeared to dispute the concept that in a contract there must be consideration.

(e) Denning adopted his famous common-sense approach in *Thornton* v *Shoe Lane Parking* [1971] 1 All ER 686, CA.

(f) Denning's judgments were written in clear and comprehensible English.

(g) Despite the simplicity of his language, the ideas and concepts he expressed were often extremely complex and challenged the rigidity imposed by the common law.

1 Which judicial achievements is the text about?

2 Where do you expect to find the answers to the Hadford University assignment?
Write 1, 2 or 3 next to the topic sentence.

3 What do you expect to find in the other paragraph(s)?

F Read the text on the opposite page and check your ideas. See *Skills bank*

HADFORD *University*

Faculty: Law

Assignment

Do some research into the people who have had the greatest influence on the law. Make notes to address these points for each person:

1 What legal problems did this person try to address?

2 How were his judgments received by the profession?

3 What effect have his judgments had on the way the law operates today?

The judicial achievements of Lord Denning

Alfred Thompson, Lord Denning was one of the greatest judges working in the English legal system during the 20th century. Many of his judicial decisions have had a wide impact on many aspects of the law. He became famous for his landmark judgments. He established the principle of equitable estoppel and ensured that the small print on the back of a ticket could not be used by companies to avoid their legal obligations.

Denning also made some controversial judgments that some jurists believe damaged his reputation. Despite strong evidence in their favour, he did not allow an appeal by a group of Irish republicans, known as the Birmingham Six, against their conviction on terrorism charges, on the grounds that, to do so, would indicate the police investigating the crime had been corrupt. The police had, in fact, interfered with the evidence and after a long campaign the men were eventually released. They had been wrongfully imprisoned for more than ten years.

As Master of the Rolls, the most senior judge in the Civil Division of the Court of Appeal, Denning challenged the principle of *stare decisis* (judicial binding precedent). He believed that if a rule had been made by the Court of Appeal, it could also be changed by it. In the well-known case of *Spartan Steel and Alloys Ltd* v *Martin and Co* [1972] 3 All ER 557, CA Denning did not follow precedent and based his judgment on a thorough analysis of the facts of the case.

In *Central London Property Trust Ltd* v *High Trees House Ltd* [1947] KB 130 Denning appeared to dispute the concept that in a contract there must be consideration. The facts of the case were that the plaintiffs rented out their property, a block of flats in central London, to the defendants at a fixed rent agreed by both parties. After this agreement was made, World War II started and the defendants found it difficult to find tenants for the flats. The plaintiffs promised to cut the annual rent by half. After the war ended, the flats again became fully occupied and the plaintiffs wanted to receive the original rent. The court decided that they were entitled to the full rent but starting only from the end of the war. Denning argued that the plaintiffs' promise to reduce the rent stopped them from enforcing the original contract, even though the defendants had not given any consideration. This promise estopped, or prevented, the plaintiffs from enforcing their strict legal rights.

Denning adopted his famous common-sense approach in *Thornton* v *Shoe Lane Parking* [1971] 1 All ER 686, CA. The plaintiff bought a ticket to park his car in the defendants' car park. The ticket was issued subject to the conditions displayed on a notice in the car park. These conditions, in very small print, stated that the owners of the car park were not liable for any injuries caused to their customers. The plaintiff was injured, partly as a result of the defendants' negligence. The court held that the plaintiff was not bound by the conditions. Denning stated that: 'In order to give sufficient notice, it would need to be printed in red ink with a red hand pointing to it.' The defendants could not avoid their duty of care unless they informed their customers about the conditions for parking in a clear and appropriate way.

Denning's judgments were written in clear and comprehensible English. They were very different from the legalistic language used by many of his fellow judges. The reasons for his decisions could be understood by people who were not lawyers. One of his most famous judgments was in *Miller* v *Jackson* [1977] QB 966, CA in what became known as 'the cricket case'. This involved the traditional English summer sport. A family that had just bought a house next to a cricket ground complained that cricket balls were being hit into their garden and disturbing their right to its peaceful enjoyment. Denning began in the following way:

> In summertime village cricket is the delight of everyone. Nearly every village has its own cricket field where young men play and old men watch. In the village of Linz in County Durham [in the north of England], they have their own ground where they have played these last 70 years … yet now after these 70 years a Judge of the High Court has ordered they must not play there anymore.

Despite the simplicity of his language, the ideas and concepts he expressed were often extremely complex and challenged the rigidity imposed by the common law. Although some of his decisions were overturned by the House of Lords, many of the causes he championed were written into statutes. Examples of these are the right of deserted wives to remain in the marital home, and the concept that a person who makes a negligent misstatement cannot later rely on it.

A Study the words in box a. They are all from the text in Lesson 2.

1 Give two meanings of each word.

2 Check with your dictionary.

B Study the words in box b. They are all from the text in Lesson 2.

1 What is the base word in each case? What part of speech is the base word?

2 Does the prefix/suffix change the part of speech?

3 How does it change the meaning?

C Look back at the topic sentences on page 16. Don't look at the text on page 17. What information comes after each topic sentence? Suggest possible content.
Example:

> Denning adopted his famous common-sense approach in *Thornton* v *Shoe Lane Parking* [1971] 1 All ER 686, CA.

The facts of the case; how Denning used common sense.

D Write a summary of the text on page 17. Paraphrase the topic sentences. Add extra information and examples. See *Skills bank*

A Can you remember all the people who have made a contribution to the development of the law from Lesson 2? What were their main achievements?

B The lecturer has asked you to research *judicial precedent*.

1 What do you understand by the term?

2 Think of good research questions before you read the text.

3 Look quickly at the text on the opposite page. What is the best way to record information while you are reading?

C Study the text on the opposite page.

1 Highlight the topic sentences.

2 Read each topic sentence. What will you find in the rest of the paragraph?

3 Which paragraph(s) will probably answer each research question? Read those paragraphs and make notes.

4 Have you got all the information you need? If not, read other paragraphs.

D Use the Internet to research the judicial achievements of one of the people from the list in Lesson 2. Use the same research questions as in Lesson 2.

1 Make notes.

2 Write a series of topic sentences which summarize your findings.

3 Report back to the other students. Read out each topic sentence then add extra details.

Judicial precedent

Lord Denning

Judicial precedent can be defined as the principle whereby judges are required to follow the decisions made in previous cases which have sufficient similarity. Cases decided by lower courts must always follow the precedent set by higher courts. The aim of *stare decisis* (Latin for 'the decision must stand') is to provide consistency and predictability in the decision-making process of various courts.

The judgment may fall into two parts: the *ratio decidendi* (the reason for the decision) and the *obiter dictum* (something said by the way). The *ratio decidendi* always applies to the precise facts of the case and is binding. In other words, it sets a precedent that must be followed. The *obiter dictum* is where a judge speculates on what might have happened if the facts had been different. This part of the judgment is persuasive rather than binding and so does not have to be followed. In the *High Trees* case, Lord Denning decided that the plaintiffs were entitled to payment of the full rent only after the war had ended. This was the *ratio decidendi.* He speculated that the plaintiffs would not be entitled to the full rent from the start of the war as they had promised to cut the rent by half to ease the defendants' financial difficulties. However, as this was not based on the strict facts of the case, this part of the decision was *obiter dictum.*

The court hierarchy dictates the way in which judicial precedent operates. Under section 3(1) of the European Communities Act, the decisions made on matters of European Community Law are binding on all courts within the English legal system, including the Supreme Court. If matters of European Community Law are not involved, the Supreme Court is the highest court in the land. The Supreme Court is bound by its own decisions unless the court decides in a particular case that this is not right. This was laid down by Lord Gardiner in the *Practice Statement* in 1966. Supreme Court decisions are binding on all lower courts.

The Court of Appeal (Civil Division) must follow the decisions of the Supreme Court even if it is considered wrong to do so. In *Young* v *Bristol Aeroplane*

Co Ltd [1944] KB 718, CA, the Court of Appeal decided it is also bound by its own decisions except where:

- previous decisions in the Court of Appeal conflict. It must then decide which one to follow.

- a decision of its own conflicts with a Supreme Court decision, even if that decision has not been expressly overruled by the Supreme Court.

- a decision of its own was made *per incuriam*; in other words, by mistake.

The Court of Appeal (Criminal Division) generally has the same rules of *stare decisis* as the Civil Division. However, because decisions might affect the liberty of the individual, the rules of precedent are not followed as rigidly. This principle was laid down in *R* v *Taylor* [1950] 2KB 368, where it was held that if questions involving the liberty of a subject had either been misapplied or misunderstood, the court should reconsider the decision.

The High Court is bound by decisions of the Supreme Court and the Court of Appeal. It is not bound by previous High Court decisions. However, these are of strong persuasive authority and are usually followed. Decisions of High Court judges are binding in the county courts. Decisions made on points of law by judges in the Crown Court are not binding. They are only of persuasive authority, so other Crown Court judges need not follow them. The decisions of the county courts and the magistrates' courts are not binding.

Courts can avoid following a binding precedent in a case by using a legal device called 'distinguishing'. Cases can be distinguished on either the facts or the points of law. In a case involving a joint enterprise, where two people take part in a robbery, and in the course of the robbery one of the people kills the person they are stealing from, the person who does not actually *do* the killing may still be liable if he could foresee that this action was likely to follow. If someone is armed with a gun, murder is more foreseeable than if someone is armed only with a stick. In *R* v *Powell (Anthony) and English* [1999] 1 AC 1, HL, Lord Hutton made this distinction.

Judicial precedent provides stability and consistency within the legal system. However, there are cases where its rigidity has led to injustices. The arguments are whether these injustices should be rectified by Parliament through a change in the law, or whether it is up to judges to use their skills to avoid a precedent where it would, in the circumstances of the case, be unjust to follow it.

Using your English–English dictionary

This kind of dictionary helps you actually **learn** English.

Using headwords and parts of speech

1 Find the correct **headword**.
   These **bold** words in a dictionary are in alphabetical order. Look at the words on the top left and top right of the double page. Find a word which comes just before and after your word.

2 Find the correct **meaning**.
   If there are different meanings of the word, they appear in a numbered list. Look at all the meanings before you choose the correct one in context.

3 Find the correct **part of speech**.
   Sometimes the same headword appears more than once, followed by a small number. This means the word has more than one part of speech, e.g., *n* and *v*. Work out the part of speech before you look up a word. Clues:
   - Nouns come after articles (*a/an/the*) or adjectives.
   - Verbs come after nouns or pronouns.

Learning to pronounce words

The symbols after the headword show you how to pronounce the word. Learn these symbols (the key is usually at the front or the back of the dictionary).

The little line in the symbols shows you how to stress the word.
Example:
/dʒuːˈdɪʃ(ə)l/ but /ˈdʒʌstɪs/

Learning to use words correctly in context

Nouns can be **countable** or **uncountable**. This information is important for using articles and verb forms (e.g., *is/are*) correctly. Look for the symbol [**C**] or [**U**].

Some verbs need an object. They are **transitive**. Some verbs don't need an object. They are **intransitive**. This information is important for making good sentences. Look for the symbol [**T**] or [**I**].

Some words can be spelt in **British** English (e.g., *offence, centre*) or **American** English (e.g., *offense, center*). Choose the correct spelling for the text you are working on.

Doing reading research

Before you start reading ...

- Think of research questions. In other words, ask yourself: *What must I find out from my research?*
- Look at headings, sub-headings, illustrations. Look for patterns or variations in presentation, e.g., a series of dates; words in **bold** or *italic* script. Think: *What information do they give me?*
- Decide how to record information from your reading. Choose one or more methods of note-taking. See Unit 1 *Skills bank*

While you are reading ...

- Highlight the topic sentences.
- Think: *Which paragraph(s) will probably give me the answer to my research questions?*
- Read these paragraph(s) first.
- Make notes.

After reading ...

- Think: *Did the text answer all my research questions?*
- If the answer is no, look at other paragraphs to see if the information is there.

Using topic sentences to summarize

The topic sentences of a text normally make a good basis for a summary. Follow this procedure:

- Locate the topic sentences.
- Paraphrase them – in other words, rewrite them in your own words so that the meaning is the same. Do not simply copy them. (This is a form of plagiarism.)
- Add supporting information – once again, in your own words.

Example:

Paraphrase of topic sentence	*Lord Denning used simple and straightforward language in his judgments.*
Supporting information and examples (summarized)	*For example, he introduced a judgment in a famous case with: 'In summertime village cricket is the delight of everyone.'*

- Check your summary. Check that the ideas flow logically. Check spelling and grammar. If your summary is short, it may be just one paragraph. Divide a longer summary into paragraphs.

3 CRIMES AND CIVIL WRONGS

A Discuss these questions.

  1 What types of tort are commonly recognized by lawyers?

  2 What is the main difference between a tort and a crime?

B Study the photos on the opposite page. Decide the type of wrong being committed in each picture. Use words from box a.

> **a** battery burglary
> deception defamation
> false imprisonment fraud
> homicide libel negligence
> slander theft trespass

C Study the words in box a.

  1 Put the words into two groups. Explain your choice.

  2 Where is the main stress in each multi-syllable word?

D Complete each sentence with a word from box a. Change the form if necessary (e.g., change a noun into an adjective).

  1 The government minister stated that there was no truth in the article and threatened to sue the newspaper for making a _____ or defamatory statement.

  2 The employees claimed that the owners of the factory were _____ because they failed to ensure their safety.

  3 If people _____ on your property you have the right to use reasonable force to evict them.

  4 The definition of _____ is the dishonest appropriation of property belonging to another with the intention permanently to deprive.

  5 If you repeat that blatant lie in public again I will have no alternative but to sue you for

  _____ .

  6 Murder is the most serious form of _____ .

  7 The intentional striking of someone that results in harm is known as _____ .

E Study the words in box b. Find the prefix and try to work out the meaning in each case.

> **b** | defame | disorder | insanity | malpractice | misconduct | nonfeasance |
> | deport | disgrace | incapacity | malfeasance | misfeasance | noncompliance |
> | deviate | disinterested | insolvency | malicious | misinterpret | nonsense |

F Complete each sentence with a word from box b. Change the form if necessary.

  1 The employee was sacked for gross _____ after stealing a laptop.

  2 Scottish law does not differentiate between libel and slander, and all cases are known simply as

  _____ .

  3 He pleaded not guilty to murder by reason of _____ .

  4 The legal term for a tort where a person fails to do something they should have done is

  _____ .

  5 In cases of _____ , a professional has failed to carry out his or her duties to the standard expected, and as a result the client has suffered a loss.

  6 Police can now issue on-the-spot fines for minor offences of public _____ .

SPORT

Cop saw Melv... beaten in the fi... rowdy play re... team to 9 men... goal by De Wi... Castle's keepe... alised. Anothe... card for Stewart... could be on th... list by the end... son. Necastle p... after some scr... which resulted... ner, Okubango... elled the... Bolton surged t... score two more... succsion, a... taken by Ro... lowed by a fin... strike by De W... last two... Newcastle will... ed if they loos... Rotherham ne...
• *Keith Jones*

NO RIGHT OF WAY
INTRUDERS WILL BE PROSECUTED

TOP MANAGER *Liar*

Roe-Roe's new Manager **Jack Miller** has been accused of embezzlement in connection with club funds, it was reported today. Roehampton's Board of Directors has suspended Millar as Manager following disclosures to the Police by Treasurer Terrence Marks. Millar has repeated lied about his activities branded a common thief. Funds in excess of £25K are said to have been mis-appropriated by Miller. Metropolitan Police have refused bail after Miller became violent during his arrest at the ground on Saturday. He will face court procedings next week. His extravagant lifestyle had been a cause for suspicion for some-

Premier League
Jon Ebbs
P.Thompson
Jason Smith
Paul Anford
Mike Snow
F. Johnson
Terry James
Matt Truskett
K.Lock
Alan Dock
R.Mantle
M.LeCrusier
Henri Guy
Mick Haines
John Barnes
Martin Feld
Eric Long
Xavier LeBlanc
Tom Bridge

A Study the slides from a lecture.

   1 What do you expect to learn in this lecture? Make a list of points.

   2 Write down some key words you expect to hear.

   3 Check the pronunciation of the key words, with other students or with a dictionary.

   4 How are you going to prepare for this lecture?

B Listen to Part 1 of the lecture.

   1 What exactly is the lecturer going to talk about? Tick the topic(s) you heard.

     • civil courts   ____

     • criminal courts   ____

     • characteristics of wrongdoing   ____

     • assault and battery   ____

     • trespass to goods   ____

     • injunctions   ____

     • tribunals   ____

   2 What reason does the lecturer give for talking about the court system?

   3 What might be a good way to organize notes for this lecture?

C Listen to Part 2 of the lecture.

   1 What is the main idea of this section?

   2 Is *trespass* a crime or a tort?

   3 What remedy for trespass does the lecturer mention?

   4 What is the legal definition of *battery*?

   5 Where would a case of theft be tried?

   6 What do you expect to hear in the next part of the lecture?

D Listen to Part 3 of the lecture.

   1 How could you write notes for this part?

   2 What are the types of court and cases that they hear?

E Listen to Part 4 of the lecture.

   1 Check your answers to Exercise D, question 2.

   2 What will the next lecture be about?

F Listen and say whether the sentences are true or false. Explain your reasons.

   1 ____   **2** ____   **3** ____   **4** ____   **5** ____   **6** ____

HADFORD *University*

Faculty: Law

Lecture 5A
Courts in the English Legal System

Slide 1

Torts (disputes between private citizens resolved in civil courts)

  • trespass to the person

  • assault

  • battery

  • false imprisionment

  • trespass to property

Slide 2

Crimes (breaches of the law heard in criminal courts)

  • offences against the person

  • assault

  • murder

  • manslaughter

  • theft

Slide 3

3.3 Extending skills
stress within words • using information sources • reporting findings

A 🎧 Listen to some stressed syllables. Identify the word below in each case. Number each word.

Example:

You hear: *1 wrong* /rɒŋ/   You write:

assault	___	defamation	___	permanently	___
battery	___	deliberately	___	prohibitory	___
contempt	___	dishonest	___	prosecute	___
criminal	___	dispute	___	reckless	___
custodial	___	injunction	___	trespass	___
damages	___	justice	___	wrongdoing	_1_

B Where is the stress in each multi-syllable word in Exercise A?

   1 Mark the stress.

   2 Practise saying each word.

C Work in pairs or groups. Define one of the words in Exercise A.
The other student(s) must find and say the correct word.

D Before you attend a lecture you should do some research.

   1 How could you research the lecture topics on the right?

   2 What information should you record?

   3 How could you record the information?

E You are going to do some research on a particular lecture topic. You must find:

   1 a dictionary definition

   2 a legal explanation

   3 a useful Internet site

HADFORD *University*

Faculty: Law

1 Trespass to the person, goods, property

2 The European Court of Justice: a brief history

3 The duties and responsibilities of High Court judges

4 Theft

Student A

- Do some research on **theft**.
- Tell your partner about your findings.

Student B

- Do some research on **trespass to the person**.
- Tell your partner about your findings.

A You are going to listen to a lecture which extends the topic of the lecture in Lesson 2.

   1 Make a list of points from that lecture.

   2 What is the lecturer going to talk about today? (Clue: Some of you researched it in Lesson 3.)

   3 🎧 Listen to the end of the last lecture again and check your ideas.

B What are the ways in which trespass to the person can be committed?

   1 Make a list of ways. The information on the opposite page may help you.

   2 🎧 Listen to Part 1 of the lecture and check your ideas.

   3 What is a good way to make notes from this lecture? Prepare a page for your notes.

C 🎧 Listen to Part 2 of the lecture. Make notes. If necessary, ask other students for information.

D 🎧 Listen to Part 3 of the lecture. List the defences that are available to a person sued for trespass to the person.

E 🎧 Listen to the final part of the lecture. Summarize the key points.

F Imagine you had to report this lecture to a student who was absent.

   1 Study the transcript on pages 118–119. Find and underline or highlight key sections of the lecture.

   2 Find and underline key sentences from the lecture.

   3 Make sure you can say the sentences with good pronunciation.

   4 Compare your ideas in groups.

G Which trespass to the person is possibly committed by each of these actions?

   • shaking your fist in anger

   • punching someone in the face

   • locking someone up in a room

   • performing a medical operation without the patient's consent

   • using abusive language

H Match the words (1–8) to the best definition.

   1 implied — a person who makes a legal complaint against another party through the courts

   2 consent (n) — to control or limit a person's movements

   3 constrain — permission or agreement to do something

   4 intentional — an essential requirement

   5 reasonable — the cause of harm to another person

   6 necessity — based on fair and practical judgement

   7 plaintiff — communication of something that is not expressed directly

   8 infliction — where there is a plan or purpose

HADFORD *University*   **Faculty: Law**

Trespass to the person

Assault

J Lyons and Sons v *Wilkins* [1899] 1 Ch 298

Thomas v *NUM* [1985] 2 WLR 1081

Tuberville v *Savage* (1669) 86 ER 684

Slide 1

Trespass to the person

Battery

Wiffin v *Kincard* (1807) 2 Bos & PNR 471

Letang v *Cooper* [1964] 2 All ER 929, CA

Wilson v *Pringle* [1986] 2 All ER 440

Slide 2

Trespass to the person

False imprisonment

Wilkinson v *Downton* [1897] 2 QB 57

Robinson v *Balmain New Ferry* [1910] AC 295

Murray v *Ministry of Defence* [1988] 2 All ER 521, HL

Slide 3

Stress within words

Nouns, verbs, adjectives and **adverbs** are called **content words** because they carry the meaning.

One-syllable words

Some content words have **one syllable** or sound. This is always stressed.

Examples:
'tort, 'court, 'theft, 'case, 'state

Two-syllable words

Some content words have **two syllables**. Two-syllable nouns and adjectives are often stressed on the first syllable. Two-syllable verbs are often stressed on the second syllable.

Examples:

Nouns	'contract, 'justice, 'libel
Adjectives	'civil, 'legal, 'private, 'reckless
Verbs	con'sent, a'rrest, re'solve

Exceptions:

Nouns	a'ssault, de'fence
Adjectives	im'plied
Verbs	'damage, 'slander

Multi-syllable words

Some content words have **three or more syllables**. Multi-syllable words are normally stressed three syllables from the end.

Example:
O o o   o O o o   o o O o o

This is true for most words ending in:

~ize/~ise	'summarize, hy'pothesise
~sis	a'nalysis, hy'pothesis
~ate	de'liberate, 'magistrate
~ify	'testify, 'specify
~phere	'atmosphere
~ical	po'litical, 'medical
~ity	com'plicity, du'plicity
~ular	par'ticular, 'regular
~ium	de'lirium, equi'librium
~al	cus'todial, in'tentional

Exceptions:
Multi-syllable words ending in the following letters are normally stressed two syllables from the end.

~ic	spe'cific, in'trinsic
~ion	con'viction, defa'mation
~cian	poli'tician
~sion	co'mmission, poss'ession
~ent	co'herent, e'fficient

Skills bank

Getting information from other people

From the lecturer

We can sometimes ask a lecturer questions at the end of a lecture. Introduce each question in a polite or tentative way.

Examples:
Could you go over the bit about trespass to the person *again?*
I didn't quite understand what you said about assault and battery.
I wonder if you could repeat the name of the defendant in the case.
Would you mind giving the case citation *again?*

From other students

It is a good idea to ask other students after a lecture for information to complete your notes.

Examples:
What did the lecturer say about a tort?
Why did the lecturer tell that story about someone entering a house?
I didn't get the bit about courts and tribunals.

Be polite!

It sometimes sounds impolite to ask people a direct question.
We often add a polite introduction.

Examples:
Does assault always involve physical force?
→   *Do you know if assault always involves physical force?*
What does 'battery' mean?
→   *Can you remember what 'battery' means?*

Reporting information to other people

We often have to report research findings to a tutor or other students in a seminar. Make sure you can give:

- sources – books, articles, writers, publication dates
- quotes – in the writer's own words
- summary findings – in your own words

4.1 Vocabulary
computer jargon • abbreviations and acronyms • verb and noun suffixes

A Study the words and phrases in box a.

1 Which words or phrases relate to computers and the Internet? Which relate to books and libraries? Find two groups of words.

2 Find pairs of words and phrases with similar meanings, one from each group.

3 Check your ideas with the first part of *The Computer Jargon Buster* on the opposite page.

B Complete the instructions for using the Learning Resource Centre with words or phrases from box a.

C Study the abbreviations and acronyms in box b.

1 How do you say each one?

2 Divide them into two groups:

- abbreviations
- acronyms

See *Vocabulary bank*

D Test each other on the items in Exercise C.

1 What do the letters stand for in each case?

2 What do they mean?

3 Check your ideas with the second part of *The Computer Jargon Buster* on the opposite page.

E Study the nouns in box c.

1 Make a verb from each noun.

2 Make another noun from the verb.

---

a

books   browse/search   catalogue   close
cross-reference   database   electronic resources
exit/log off   hyperlink   index   library
log in/log on   look up   menu   open   page
search engine results   table of contents
web page   World Wide Web

HADFORD *University*

Learning Resource Centre

Instructions for use:

If you want to access web pages on the
_____ , you must first
_____ to the university Intranet
with your username and password. You can
use any _____ but the default is
Google. _____ for web pages by
typing one or more keywords in the search
box and clicking on **Search**, or pressing
Enter. When the results appear, click on a
_____ (highlighted in blue) to go to
the web page. Click on **Back** to return to the
results listing.

You can also use the university _____
of learning resources. Click on **Law Resources**
on the main _____ .

---

b

CAL   DVD   HTML   HTTP   ISP
LCD   MNC   PIN   ROM   URL
USB   WAN   WWW

---

c

class   computer   digit
identity   machine

Computer Weekly International magazine

The Computer Jargon Buster

There are many common words used about books and libraries which are translated into jargon words when we talk about using computers and the Internet for similar functions.

books	electronic resources
index	search engine results
cross-reference	hyperlink
catalogue	database
library	World Wide Web
table of contents	menu
look up	browse/search
page	web page
open	log in/log on
close	exit/log off

There are many abbreviations and acronyms in computing. Learn some useful ones.

Abbr./Acr.	What it stands for	What it means
CAL	computer-assisted learning	using computers to help you learn
DVD	digital versatile disk	a disk for storing data, including sound and pictures
HTML	hypertext markup language	a way to write documents so they can be displayed on a website
HTTP	hypertext transfer protocol	a set of rules for transfering files on the WWW, usually included at the beginning of a website address (e.g., http://www. ...)
ISP	Internet service provider	a company which gives individuals, companies, etc. access to the Internet
LCD	liquid crystal display	the kind of screen you get on many laptops
MNC	medium-neutral citation	a citation system used for unpublished electronic judgments; references are to paragraph not page numbers
PIN	personal identification number	a collection of numbers or letters which are used like a password to identify someone
ROM	read-only memory	a type of permanent computer or disk memory that stores information that can be read or used but not changed
URL	uniform resource locator	a website address, e.g., http://www.garneteducation.com
USB	universal serial bus	a standard way to connect things like printers and scanners to a computer
WAN	wide area network	a way of connecting computers in different places, often very far apart
WWW	World Wide Web	a huge collection of documents that are connected by hypertext links and can be accessed through the Internet

A Discuss these questions.

1 What types of organization provide access to useful information for lawyers?

2 How has the Internet helped make the law-making process more transparent?

B You are going to read a guide on using the Internet for law studies. Write three questions you want the guide to answer.

C One student wrote about accessing information on the Internet before reading the text on the opposite page. Write **A** (I agree), **D** (I disagree) or **?** (I'm not sure) next to the ideas on the right.

D Read all the topic sentences.

1 What is the structure of this text? Choose Structure A or B on the right.

2 What do you expect to find in each paragraph?

E Read the text and check your predictions.

F Answer these questions.

1 Where would you look for primary sources when conducting research?

2 Why are there no page numbers in a medium-neutral citation?

3 Which court was a case cited as *EWHC* (*Fam*) heard in?

4 Why is the House of Lords cited as *UKHL* in medium-neutral citation?

G Topics sometimes develop inside a paragraph.

1 Does the topic develop in each paragraph in the text? If so, underline the word or words which introduce the change.

2 What is the effect of the word or words on the development of the topic?

See Skills bank

You can waste a lot of time searching the web for information that is completely irrelevant. ____

Books in the library are a much more reliable source of information than the web. ____

It is much easier to do research on case law in the library rather than on the Internet. ____

It is difficult to judge whether or not the information on a blog site is correct. ____

Structure A

Para 1	Intro. to legal sources on the Internet
Para 2	Availability of access to UK legislation
Para 3	Costs of accessing case law
Para 4	Availability of secondary sources
Para 5	Using information from other sources
Para 6	Interpreting website codes

Structure B

Para 1.	Primary sources of legal information
Para 2.	Different types of statute
Para 3.	How to pay for legal information
Para 4.	Advantages of using text books
Para 5.	Controlling information
Para 6.	Finding countries on the web

HADFORD *University*   **Library Guides**

Using the Internet for law studies

The Internet holds a huge store of information that is useful for lawyers and law students. This information comes from a wide variety of sources such as the government, the courts, legal organizations, special interest groups, the media and individuals. However, to avoid wasting a huge amount of time on fruitlessly searching irrelevant domains, you need to know how to choose the best and most appropriate websites. When doing research, you will need to go to what are known as *primary sources* – original texts such as Acts of Parliament and verbatim, or word-for-word, reports of judgments in the Court of Appeal or the House of Lords or Supreme Court. You will also need to read *secondary sources*, such as legal text books, law journals and authoritative newspapers.

Primary sources

In the UK, legislation from all jurisdictions (England and Wales, Scotland and Northern Ireland) passed after 1988 is now freely available. Judgments after 1996 from the House of Lords (Supreme Court from 2009) and the Court of Appeal are also available without subscription. In addition, there is free access to many official UK government sources. These sites contain policy statements, consultation papers and other useful documents. At a European level, the European Parliament has gone further and made all European Community legislation available. European Case law is also freely available from the European Court of Justice and the European Court of Human Rights.

The British and Irish Legal Information Institution (BAILII) is building a site to provide free access to important and useful cases. This includes cases not only from England and Wales and Ireland but from other jurisdictions such as Hong Kong and Australia. Unfortunately, this site is taking time to develop so the reports on some of the cases listed are not yet accessible. In the meantime, Hadford University Library pays a subscription to the Westlaw UK site which has law reports dating back to 1865.

Secondary sources

Some law text books and journals are available free online. These include mostly older text books and, for example, *The Lawyer* journal. Most publishers also have websites to support their text books which provide regular updates and useful links. However, the most authoritative journals (e.g., the *Oxford Journal of Legal Studies* and *The Cambridge Law Journal*) are usually subscription only. Newspapers can also provide an excellent source of up-to-date information on recent cases and changes to the law. *The Times* and *The Guardian* have special legal sections. Many professional organizations, such as The Law Society and The Bar Council in the UK and The American Society of International Law, have their own websites.

There are also a number of sites for special interest groups, as well as individually written blogs. Remember, though, that material such as this on the Internet is not checked and is often written in a subjective way. There is no control over what people can write so be very cautious about the websites you select and the information you read.

Use the URL to help you decide if the sites located by the search engine are likely to be useful. Remember to look at the domain or organizational code as well as the country the site originated from. Many URLs, though, especially from the United States (.us), do not include the country code.

Citation

Since January 2001, as a result of cases being made available on the Internet, the way cases are cited has changed. There is now a system known as *medium-neutral citation.* Cases are cited by the names of the parties (e.g., *Smith* v *Jones*) and the medium-neutral citation which must include the year [2001], the jurisdiction (e.g., EW = England and Wales), the court, such as the Court of Appeal (CA), the division of the court (civ = civil; crim = criminal; ch = chancery), and the official reference number. For example: *Grobbelaar* v *News Group Ltd* [2001] EWCA Civ 1213

Cases heard in the House of Lords are not cited with a reference number but with the number of the case heard. So *Johnson (A.P.)* v *Unisys Ltd* [2001] UKHL 13 was the thirteenth case to be heard in the House of Lords since the introduction of the system.

Medium-neutral citation does not use page numbers to locate a reference. This is now done through numbered paragraphs. Lawyers will say 'at paragraph 17' rather than 'on page 3' when they want to highlight a particular point made in a case.

A Discuss these questions.

1 You want to find out about medium-neutral citation in law cases. Where would you look for the information? Why?

2 What keywords would you use to make this search? Why?

B Your search produces 50 results. How can you select the most useful ones without reading all of them? Look at the list of criteria on the right and put a tick or '?'.

C You have some more research tasks (below). Choose up to three keywords or phrases for each search.

1 What are the defences to the tort of trespass to the person?

2 What is the maximum custodial sentence a magistrates' court can pass?

3 What types of cases are heard in the county courts in England and Wales?

D Go to a computer and try out your chosen keywords.

Criteria for choosing to read a result

It contains all of my keywords. ____

The document comes from a journal. ____

It is in the first ten. ____

It has this year's date. ____

It is a large document. ____

The website address ends in .org ____

The website address ends in .edu ____

The website address contains .ac ____

It is a PDF file. ____

It refers to law. ____

It refers to a person I know (of). ____

It refers to an organization I know (of). ____

A What information is contained in the results listings of a search engine?

1 Make a list.

2 Check with the results listings on the opposite page.

B Scan the results listings. What keywords were entered?

C Answer these questions.

1 What abbreviations or acronyms can you find in the results?

2 Where is each website address?

3 Where is the size of each document?

4 Which are PDF documents?

5 Which documents have dates?

6 Why are the words in different colours?

7 Which results have all the keywords?

8 Which results come from educational sites?

9 What does _similar pages_ mean?

10 What does _cached_ mean?

D Continue your research on medium-neutral citation by entering the keywords into a search engine and accessing three of the results. Compare your findings with other students.

E Choose the most interesting result. Write a paragraph about the information you discovered. Develop the topic within the paragraph with discourse markers and stance markers.

Google

Sign in

Web   Images   Groups   News   Froogle   Maps   **more »**

(Search) Advanced Search
Preferences

Web   Results **1 - 4** of about **34,300,000** for "**medium neutral citation**" [definition]. (0.12 seconds)

[PDF]
1 Media **Neutral Citation**
File Format: PDF/Adobe Acrobat - View as HTML
Media **neutral citation** is a method of citing an unreported judgment which does not discriminate between ...
media **neutral citation** formats for judgments. ...
wwwlib.murdoch.edu.au/guides/arts/law/6.pdf - Similar pages

2 **Medium Neutral Citation** in Treaties and Related Documents
The Commonwealth Government has adopted the **medium neutral citation** system for the Australian Treaties
Series on both the Australian Treaties Database (ATD) ...
www.dfat.gov.au/treaties/making/citations.html - 13k - Cached - Similar pages

3 N.D.R.Ct. 1. 6 **Medium-Neutral** Case **Citations**
Rule 11.6 was adopted, effective March 5, 1997, subject to comment, to implement the use of **medium-neutral**
case **citations** in North Dakota. ...
www.court.state.nd.us/court/rules/ndroc/rule11.6.htm - 5k - Cached - Similar pages

[PDF]
4 North Dakota **Neutral Citation Format** "Rule 11.6 **Medium-neutral ...**
File Format: PDF/Adobe Acrobat - View as HTML
use of **medium-neutral** case **citations** in North Dakota. "For Illustrative Purposes. Cite to a North Dakota
Supreme Court Opinion published prior to January 1, ...
www.alwd.org/cm/cmAppendices/FirstEditionAppendices/North%20Dakota.pdf - Similar pages

5 Encouraging the use of **medium neutral citation** - [2005] CompLRes 10
Each year, when explaining **medium neutral citation** to our Legal Research ... First what is a **medium neutral
citation**? It is a **citation** that does not depend ...
bar.austlii.edu.au/au/other/CompLRes/2005/10.html - 22k - Cached - Similar pages

6 CCC - A **Neutral Citation** Standard for Case Law
[HCA] High Court of Australia, "Paragraph Numbers in High Court of Australia Judgments and the use of
"Medium Neutral" Citations", ...
www.lexum.umontreal.ca/ccc-ccr/neutr/neutr.jur_en.html - 49k - Cached - Similar pages

7 **Citation** of case law - Newcastle Law School - Newcastle University
Cases reported since the introduction of **medium neutral citation** will conform to the ... If a case has a
medium neutral citation you may use that alone, ...
www.ncl.ac.uk/nuls/lectures/legwrit/cite4.htm - 19k - Cached - Similar pages

8 Basic Legal **Citation**: § 1-600 (2005)
The AALL has gone further and published a Universal **Citation** Guide. This guide sets out a blueprint for courts
designing **medium-neutral citation** schemes for ...
www.law.cornell.edu/citation/1-600.htm - 9k - Cached - Similar pages

9 Legal Citation: Public domain or **medium neutral citations**
Legal **Citation** Style Guide Online, with abbreviation tables, sample **citations**, and software to automate
Bluebook and ALWD **citation** styles.
www.legalcitation.net/qneutralcitations.htm - 4k - Cached - Similar pages

10 Electronic Law Journals - JILT 2000 (3) - Foster
By '**medium neutral citation** reform', I mean a citation form that is assigned at ... I would group obstacles to
medium neutral citation form into four types: ...
www2.warwick.ac.uk/fac/soc/law/elj/jilt/2000_3/foster/ - 47k - Cached - Similar pages

Understanding abbreviations and acronyms

An **abbreviation** is a shorter version of something. For example, PC /piːsiː/ is an abbreviation for *personal computer* or (in a legal context) *Privy Council*.

An **acronym** is similar to an abbreviation, but it is pronounced as a word. For example, ASBO /ˈæzbəʊ/ is an acronym for *Anti-Social Behaviour Order*.

We normally write an abbreviation or acronym with **capital letters**, although the full words may have lower case letters.

We **pronounce** the vowel letters in **abbreviations** in this way:

A	/eɪ/
E	/iː/
I	/aɪ/
O	/əʊ/
U	/juː/

We normally **pronounce** the vowel letters in **acronyms** in this way:

A	/æ/
E	/e/
I	/ɪ/
O	/ɒ/
U	/ʌ/

Common suffixes

Suffixes for verbs

There are some common verb suffixes.

Examples:

~ize	computerize, legitimize, specialize
~ify	identify, modify, specify
~ate	integrate, delegate
~en	frighten, widen

When you learn a new noun or adjective, find out how you can make it into a verb.

Suffixes for nouns

There are many suffixes for nouns. But verbs ending in ~ize, ~ify and ~ate form nouns with ~ation.

Examples:

Verb	Noun	
~ize	~ization	computerization, specialization
~ify	~ification	modification, specification
~ate	~ation	integration, delegation

Developing ideas in a paragraph

Introducing the topic

In a text, **a new paragraph** signals the start of **a new topic**.

The topic is given in the **topic sentence**, which is at or near the beginning of the paragraph. The topic sentence gives the **topic**, and also makes a **comment** about the topic.

Example:
Since January 2001, as a result of cases being made available on the Internet, the way cases are cited has changed.
The **topic** is *the way cases are cited* which, in this case, is medium-neutral citation.
The **comment** is *as a result of cases being made available on the Internet.*
The sentences that follow then expand or explain the topic sentence.

Example:
There is now a system known as medium-neutral citation. Cases are cited by the names of the parties and the medium-neutral citation which must include the year, the jurisdiction and the official reference number.

Developing the topic

Within a paragraph, ideas often develop beyond the comment.
This development is often shown by:
* a **discourse marker**: *but, however*, etc.
* a **stance marker**: *unfortunately*, etc.

Examples:
*Some law books are available free online. **However**, these tend to be older texts. There are a number of sites for special interest groups. **Unfortunately**, a lot of the information is written in a very subjective way.*

Discourse markers generally make a connection between the previous information and what comes next. They mainly introduce **contrasts** or **additional information**.

Stance markers show the **attitude** of the writer to the information, i.e., whether he/she is surprised, pleased, unhappy, etc. about the information.

Recording and reporting findings

When you do research, record information about the source. Refer to the source when you report your findings.

Examples:
According to Lord Denning MR in Miller *v* Jackson, ...
According to Digman and Lowry in their book Company Law *(2006),* ...
As the writer of the article on The Guardian Unlimited *(March 4, 2008) says,* ...

You should give the full information about the source in your reference list or bibliography. For more information about this, see Unit 10 *Skills bank*.

5 THEFT 1: THE THEFT ACT

5.1 Vocabulary word sets: synonyms, antonyms, etc.

A Look at texts on the right. What is the writer saying in each case?

B Look at the photographs on the opposite page.
  1 Where would you see each of these signs?
  2 What offence is each of these signs trying to prevent?

C Study the words in the blue box.
  1 Find words with similar meanings.
  2 What part of speech is each word?

> accused   act   be aware of   behave
> component   concern   create   crime
> defendant   deprive of   element   establish
> give back   involve   keep from   know
> offence   return   steal   take

D Study the Hadford University handout on this page.
  1 Find a word in the blue box for each blue word or phrase. Change the form if necessary.
  2 Find another word in the handout for each red word.

E Read the statements from court cases below. Rewrite each statement in your own words.
  Examples:
  1 *He is innocent of the crime.*
  2 *The property was owned by someone else.*

  1 He isn't guilty of the crime.
  2 The property didn't belong to the defendant.
  3 He didn't act dishonestly.
  4 She didn't mean to keep the property.
  5 He didn't intend to steal the car.
  6 She didn't permanently deprive her friend of the car.
  7 He didn't take the money from the till.
  8 They weren't aware that she owned the property.

Yes, as through this world I've wandered
I've seen lots of funny men;
Some will rob you with a six-gun,
And some with a fountain pen.

Lyrics from a song by Woody Guthrie,
recorded at RCA Studios, Camden, N.J, 26th Apr 1940

A man who has never gone to school may steal from a freight train, but if he has a university education he may steal the whole railroad.

Theodore Roosevelt
26th President of the USA

HADFORD *University*

Faculty: Law

Lecture: Introduction to theft

Theft is not …

- … the same as burglary. This is only a small part of theft.
- … just about stealing property. It involves many other related activities.

So what is it?

Section 1(1) of the Theft Act 1968 creates the offence of theft. It states:

'A person is guilty of theft if he dishonestly appropriates property belonging to another with the intention of permanently depriving the other of it.'

The components of theft are:

The *actus reus* of the offence. This states that the defendant:
  1 takes
  2 one or more items
  3 owned by another person.

The *mens rea* which consists of the defendant acting:
  1 dishonestly, and
  2 meaning to keep the items forever.

A possible defence against a charge of theft is that you did not know the property belonged to another party, or that you intended to return the property.

A You are going to hear a lecture about the key concepts in theft.

  1 Look at the lecture slides. What will the lecturer talk about? Make a list of topics.

  2 Write your own definition of theft.

B 🎧 Listen to Part 1 of the lecture. How will the lecture be organized? Number these topics.

- case law   ____
- components of theft   ____
- defences to a charge of theft   ____
- legal definition   ____
- offences of theft   ____

C Study the topics in Exercise B and the slides on the right.

  1 Write some key words for each topic.

  2 What is a good way to make notes?

  3 Make an outline for your notes.

D 🎧 Listen to Part 2 of the lecture.

  1 Add information to your outline notes.

  2 Which of the topics in Exercise B are discussed? In what order?

  3 Patents and trademarks are mentioned in the lecture. What are they an example of?

E 🎧 Listen to Part 3 of the lecture. Make notes.

  1 Which topic in Exercise B is mentioned?

  2 Which topic has not been mentioned?

  3 What defence does Anna have if she believes Jill gave her a watch (but then Jill says she only lent it to Anna)?

  4 What is the lecturer talking about when she loses her place?

  5 Give two ways in which, according to the Theft Act, a person does not act dishonestly.

F The lecturer used these words and phrases. Match synonyms.

  1 assumption   use *or* part with

  2 intangible   exact

  3 treat   deal with

  4 dispose of   without paying attention to

  5 regardless   invisible

  6 precise   agreement

  7 consent   taking

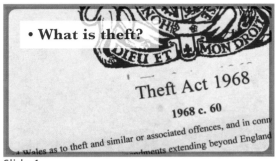
Slide 1

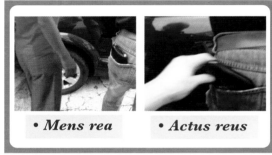
Slide 2

Slide 3

Slide 4

Slide 5

5.3 Extending skills
note-taking symbols • stress within words • lecture language

A Look at the student notes on the right. They are from the lecture in Lesson 2.

1 What do the symbols and abbreviations mean?

2 The notes contain some mistakes. Find and correct them.

3 Make the corrected notes into a spidergram.

B 🎧 Listen to the final part of the lecture (Part 4).

1 Complete your notes.

2 Why does the lecture have to stop?

3 What is the research task?

C 🎧 Listen to some stressed syllables. Identify the word below in each case. Number each word.

Example: You hear: *1 ter* /tɜː/

You write:

appropriate _____	defence _____	interpret **/**
assignment _____	definition _____	precedent _____
assumption _____	deprive _____	property _____
component _____	intangible _____	statutory _____

D Study the extract from the lecture on the right.

1 Think of one word for each space.

2 🎧 Listen and check your ideas.

3 Match words or phrases from the blue box below with each word or phrase from the lecture.

4 Think of other words or phrases with similar meanings.

> as I was saying   basically   clearly   crucial
> in fact   in other words   obviously
> of course   possibly   probably
> some people say   that is to say
> we can see that

E Discuss the research task set by the lecturer.

1 What kind of information should you find?

2 Where can you find this information?

Student notes:

3) Components
AR = guilty mind
    approp./property/belonging to another
MR = guilty deed
    a) acting dishonestly
    b) with intention
    c) perm. deprive
4) Defences
Theft = 'dishonestly approp.'
∴ defence = 'I was not dishon.'
def. in TA s2: 'not dishon.' =
    1. has right
    2. would have consent
    3. no owner
    4. willing to pay

Lecture extract:

_____ , the Theft Act 1968 is _____ one of the most important laws on the statute book. So, *it* _____ *that* the courts must ensure that cases involving theft are properly interpreted. *What I* _____ *is*, they are interpreted in the way in which Parliament intended. _____ , the courts have had to interpret a number of key words, which have at times caused judges some difficulty. Anyway, *to return to the main* _____ , it's _____ to identify the basic components that make up the crime of theft. _____ , it is the aim of all judges to interpret the statute in a just and fair way.

A Study the information on the opposite page.

   1 What does it show?

   2 Where do you think the information has come from?

B 🎧 Listen to some extracts from a seminar about judicial interpretation of the Theft Act.

   1 What is wrong with the contribution of the last speaker in each case? Choose from the following:

- it is irrelevant
- the student interrupts
- the student doesn't contribute anything to the discussion
- it is not polite
- the student doesn't explain the relevance

   2 What exactly does the student say, in each case?

   3 What should the student say or do, in each case?

C 🎧 Listen to some more extracts from the same seminar.

   1 How does the second speaker make an effective contribution? Choose from the following:

- by making clear how the point is relevant
- by bringing in another speaker
- by asking for clarification
- by paraphrasing to check understanding
- by giving specific examples to help explain a point

   2 What exactly does the student say, in each case?

   3 What other ways do you know of saying the same things?

D Make a table of **Do**'s (helpful ways) and **Don't**s (unhelpful ways) of contributing to seminar discussions.

Do's	Don'ts
ask politely for information	demand information from other students

E Work in groups.

   1 The teacher will ask you to look at case A or B on the opposite page. Study the information about the case carefully.

   2 Complete your own spidergram for the case, identifying:

- the important facts of the case
- the relevant section(s) in the Theft Act
- the judgment
- the reasons for the judgment, and the precedents which have been established

   3 Conduct a seminar. Focus on the reasons why the case is of significant legal importance.

F Present the key information about your case to the other group.

R v Gomez [1993] AC 442, HL

Crime: Theft – Dishonest appropriation.

Shop employee obtained authority by deceit to supply customer with goods against stolen cheques knowing that cheques were stolen.

Facts: The defendant, the assistant manager of a shop, was approached by a customer who wanted to acquire goods in exchange for two stolen cheques. Knowing that the cheques were stolen, the defendant (the assistant manager) deceived the shop manager into authorizing the sale of the goods to the customer in exchange for the cheques.

Statute: Theft Act 1968, sections 1(1), 3(1)

Judicial interpretation: appropriation

Judgment: Court of first instance: convicted defendant of theft. Court of Appeal (Criminal Division): quashed conviction. House of Lords, on appeal by the Crown: allowed appeal – defendant rightly convicted of theft.

Reasons: An act expressly or impliedly authorized by the owner of goods or consented to by him could amount to an appropriation of the goods within section 1(1) of the Theft Act 1968 where such authority or consent had been obtained by deception.

R v Lawrence [1972] AC 626, HL

Crime: Theft – Dishonest appropriation.

Taxi driver obtained a much higher fare than was justified.

Facts: Lawrence was a taxi driver. A foreign student hailed his cab and asked to be taken to a hotel. The real fare was approximately 30 pence. The passenger gave him a pound (100 pence) but Lawrence said that it was not enough. The passenger then offered Lawrence his wallet, and asked him to take the right amount. He took six pounds, which was about 20 times as much as the fare justified.

Statute: Theft Act 1968, section 1

Judicial interpretation: appropriation

Judgment: Court of Appeal (Criminal Division): found defendant guilty of theft.

Reasons: Lawrence's defence was that he had not appropriated any money within the terms of the Theft Act 1968, because – although he may have been dishonest – the full conditions for guilt ('dishonest appropriation') were not met. The Court of Appeal, however, decided that appropriation does not require a lack of consent to be part of the *actus reus* of crime.

Vocabulary sets

It is a good idea to learn words which go together. Why?

- It is easier to remember the words.
- You will have alternative words to use when paraphrasing research findings.
- It is not good style to repeat the same word often, so writers, and sometimes speakers, make use of words from the same set to avoid repetition.

You can create a vocabulary set with:

synonyms	words with similar meanings, e.g., *steal/appropriate/shoplift*
antonyms	words with opposite meanings, e.g., *prosecute/defend; guilty/innocent*
hypernyms	a general word for a set of words, e.g., *crime = murder, manslaughter, assault, theft*, etc. *theft = burglary, fraud, shoplifting*, etc.
linked words	e.g., *legal, the law, statute, legislation*

Stance

Speakers often use certain words and phrases to show how they feel about what they are saying.
Common stance words are:

adverbs	*arguably* *naturally* *sadly*
phrases	*of course, …* *it's essential to/that …* *we might say that …*

In many cases, different stance words and phrases are used in spoken and written language.

Spoken	Written
another thing	*additionally*
it seems	*evidently*
unfortunately	*regrettably*
believe	*contend*

Signpost language in a lecture

At the beginning of a lecture, a speaker will usually outline the talk. To help listeners understand the order of topics, the speaker will use phrases such as:

To start with I'll talk about …
Then I'll discuss …
After that, we'll look at …
I'll finish by giving a summary of …

During the lecture, the speaker may:

indicate a new topic	Moving on (from this) …
say the same thing in a different way	What I mean is, … That is to say, … To put it another way, …
return to the main point	Where was I? Oh, yes. To return to the main point … As I was saying …

Seminar language

The discussion leader may:

ask for information	What did you learn about …? Can you explain …? Can you tell me a bit more about …?
ask for opinions	What do you make of …? This is interesting, isn't it?
bring in other speakers	What do you think, Majed? What's your opinion, Evie?

Participants should:

be polite when disagreeing	Actually, I don't quite agree …
make relevant contributions	That reminds me …
give examples to explain a point	I can give an example of that.

Participants may:

agree with previous speaker	I agree, and that's why … That's true, so I think … You're absolutely right, which is why …
disagree with previous speaker	I don't think I agree with that. In my opinion … I'm not sure that's true. I think …
link to a previous speaker	As Jack said earlier, … Going back to what Leila said a while ago …
ask for clarification	Could you say more about …?
paraphrase to check understanding	So what you're saying is …
refer back to establish relevance	Just going back to …

Participants may not be sure if a contribution is new or relevant:
I'm sorry. Has anybody made the point that …?
I don't know if this is relevant.

6 THEFT 2: APPROPRIATION

6.1 Vocabulary | paraphrasing at sentence level

A Study the words in the blue box.

  1 Copy and complete the table. Put the words in one or more boxes, in each case.

  2 Build more words in the other columns.

  3 What is the special meaning of each word in law?

  4 Group the words in the blue box according to their stress pattern.

B Study the information on the opposite page. Discuss these questions using words from Exercise A.

  1 What is the fundamental difference between *theft* under section 1 of the Theft Act (Unit 5) and *taking without the owner's consent* under section 12?

  2 Under section 12, what is meant by:
    • taking?
    • a conveyance?
    • without the consent of the owner?

  3 Look at the elements of the offence on the opposite page. Which of the following is *not* likely to be classified as a conveyance? Give reasons.
    • a horse
    • a hovercraft

C Study the facts in *R v Pearce* [1973] Crim LR 321.

  1 Which elements had to be interpreted in this case?

  2 What do you think the court decided? Why?

D Two students have written about *R v Pearce*.

  1 Study A's sentences. Write one word in each space.

  2 Study B's sentences. Complete each sentence in a logical way.

E Study the facts of the cases on the opposite page.

  1 Choose one of the cases. Write a summary of the elements to be interpreted, as in Exercise D. Use your own words.

  2 Rewrite your summary in a different way.

F Study all the cases on the opposite page once more.

  1 What do you think the court decided in each case?

  2 Listen to the judgments. Do you agree with them?

---

accuse   aggravated   attempt
authority   classify   commit
conveyance   convict   decide
interpret   offence   permit   possession

Noun	Verb	Adjective
aggravation	aggravate	aggravated

 HADFORD *University*

R v Pearce [1973] Crim LR 321

Pearce took an inflatable rubber dinghy and towed it away on a trailer.

Student A

There are two _____ of the offence which have to be _____ in this case. Firstly, the court has to _____ if an inflatable rubber dinghy is a _____ . Secondly, the court needs to make a _____ as to whether towing on a trailer can be _____ as taking under the Act.

Student B

The court has to _____ on two points here. The first question is whether or not an inflatable rubber dinghy can be _____ as a _____ . The second question to be answered is whether towing on a trailer can be _____ as _____ .

The Theft Act 1968 section 12(1)

This section states that 'a person shall be guilty of an offence if, without having the consent of the owner or other lawful authority, he takes any conveyance for his or another's use or, knowing that any conveyance has been taken without such authority, drives it or allows himself to be carried in or on it.'

Elements of the offence:

Taking

The vehicle must be used as a conveyance. In other words, there must be some element of taking possession or control of the vehicle plus movement. If a person sits inside a car but does not actually drive it, this would not be taking. However, it could be seen as an attempt. If B gets into A's car without A's permission, with the intention of driving it away, but A realizes what is happening and stands in front of the car, B could be charged with attempt.

A conveyance

This means a conveyance constructed or adapted for the carriage of a person or persons, whether by land, air or water. It does not include a conveyance constructed or adapted for use only under the control of a person but not carried in it or on it. Pedal cycles are not covered under this section but by section 12(5) because the penalty for taking a cycle is a fine whereas for other types of vehicle it can be custodial.

Without the consent of the owner or other lawful authority

Section 12(7) of the Act provides that when a vehicle has been taken subject of a hiring agreement or a hire purchase agreement, a person in possession of the vehicle under such an agreement is deemed to be the owner.

Knowing that such a conveyance has been taken without consent, drives it or allows himself to be carried in or on it.

This requires knowledge that the vehicle has been taken, and the accused has either driven the vehicle or been a passenger. Section 12(6) of the Act provides that a person does **not** commit an offence under section 12 by anything done in the belief that he has the lawful authority to do it, or that he would have the owner's consent if the owner knew of his doing it and the circumstances of it.

R v Bogacki and others [1973] 2 All ER 864

The accused, who was drunk, got into a bus inside a bus garage and started the engine. The bus did not move and, after a few minutes, he got out of the bus.

R v Stokes [1982] Crim LR 695

Stokes and some friends moved his former girlfriend's car around the corner as a joke.

R v Phipps and McGill [1970] RTR 209, CA

McGill borrowed a car in order to take his wife to the railway station, to catch a train to Hastings. He agreed to return the car immediately after. His wife missed the train, and he kept the car in order to drive her there the next day.

R v Bow [1977] Crim LR 176

Bow, his brother and father were in his brother's car when it was stopped by gamekeepers. One gamekeeper blocked the road with his vehicle. Bow got into the gamekeeper's vehicle and released the handbrake so it coasted downhill. This enabled his brother to drive their car away.

A Look at Figure 1. Find the name for each type of offence in the blue box.

> a
> aggravated burglary
> robbery   theft   TWOC

B What type of offence is committed if a person:

1 takes a CD player from an empty car?

2 breaks into a house and steals some expensive jewellery?

3 steals a woman's handbag by pulling it off her shoulder?

4 hires a car for two days but brings it back after four days?

C Look at the illustration, the title, the introduction and the first sentence of each paragraph on the opposite page. What will the text be about?

D Using your ideas from Exercises A, B and C above, write some research questions.

E Read the text. Does it answer your questions?

F Study the highlighted sentences in the text. Find and underline the subject, verb and object or complement in each sentence. **See Skills bank**

G Two students paraphrased part of the text.

1 Which part of the text is it?

2 Which paraphrase is better? Why?

Figure 1: *Offences under the Theft Act 1968*

Student A

It is possible to show the difference between the offences of burglary, aggravated burglary and theft by looking at the main components of each offence.

The crime of burglary is committed if a person enters a building without the owner's consent because he wants to take something that does not belong to him.

A person commits the crime of aggravated burglary if he carries out the burglary whilst carrying an offensive weapon.

The crime of robbery is committed if someone steals something using force or with the threat of force.

Student B

To show the difference between the offences of burglary, aggravated burglary and robbery, we must identify the main elements in each offence.

In burglary, a person must go into a building as a trespasser intending to steal.

In aggravated burglary, a person must have an offensive weapon with them at the time of the offence.

Someone is guilty of robbery if he takes something and uses force or makes the person fear the use of force.

H Work in groups. Each group should write a paraphrase of a different part of the text.

It's a steal!

The general public is often unclear about the difference between burglary, aggravated burglary and robbery. In English law, the differences between the three offences have important implications in terms of the sentence a person will receive if convicted.

What is **burglary**? As lawyers, we need to be very precise about the way crimes are defined. According to section 9 of the Theft Act 1968, burglary is entering a building or part of a building with the intent to steal. You must trespass. In other words, you must have entered without permission. For example, if your neighbour has gone out and left the door unlocked, and you enter the house intending to steal their mobile phone, you are liable to be prosecuted for burglary. However, imagine a person enters a house for a cup of sugar. She finds that no one is there and then takes the item meaning to return it after going to the shops. A person who behaves in this way has probably not committed an offence under section 9 of the Act because there was no intention to steal. In the case of the phone, if there was an intention to dishonestly appropriate it, an offence has been committed. On the other hand, taking the phone to make an emergency call might be a successful defence. For example, the accused could say that he went outside to make the call because there was no reception in the house and then absent-mindedly put the phone in his pocket and forgot about it.

Under section 10(1) of the Theft Act, a person is guilty of **aggravated burglary** if he commits any burglary and at the time has with him any firearm or imitation firearm, any offensive weapon or any explosive. The courts have given a wide interpretation to section 10. In *R v Stones* [1989] 1 WLR 156 the defendant was arrested shortly after burgling a house. The police found he was carrying a kitchen knife. The defendant alleged that he only carried the knife to protect himself and claimed that he had not intended to use it in the burglary. The Court of Appeal decided that section 10 focused on the point that a person had a weapon of offence in his possession at the time of the burglary. If he was carrying a weapon, he might be tempted to use it to commit the burglary. In the later case of *R v Kelly* [1996] 1 Cr App R, CA Crim the accused broke into a house using a screwdriver. He told the householder to unplug the video and then pushed the screwdriver into his chest. The Court of Appeal held that under section 10 the screwdriver became a weapon of offence on proof that the accused meant to use it to cause injury.

Under section 8, a person is guilty of **robbery** if he steals and, immediately before or at the time of doing so, and in *order* to do so, he uses force on any person, or seeks to put any person in fear of being then and there subjected to force. The key word, of course, is force. The force must be used immediately before or at the time of the stealing. Force used after the theft is complete will not amount to a robbery. Whether force has been used against a person is a matter of fact. In practice, very little force is required in order for the offence to be classified as robbery. In *R v Dawson* [1976] Crim LR 692; Cr App R 170 the defendants crowded around the victim. One of them then pushed him, causing him to lose his balance. This enabled another of the defendants to take the victim's wallet easily. The Court of Appeal upheld the conviction for robbery.

In order to differentiate between the crimes of burglary, aggravated burglary and robbery, it is necessary to identify the key elements in each offence. In **burglary**, a person must *enter a building* as a *trespasser* with *intent* to *steal*. In **aggravated burglary**, a person must be in *possession* of any *weapon of offence* at the time he intends to carry out the burglary. A person is guilty of **robbery** if he steals and uses *force* on any person or makes any person afraid of being subjected to force. He can do this at the time of the offence or before it. The word *steal* is interpreted in the same way as the basic definition of theft. In other words, if you steal something, you dishonestly appropriate something belonging to another with the intention of permanently depriving the other of it.

Under the terms of the Theft Act, a person convicted of **robbery** or **aggravated burglary** is liable to a maximum sentence of life imprisonment. The maximum prison term for **burglary** is fourteen years.

A Study the words in box a from the text in Lesson 2.

1 What part of speech are they in the text?

2 Find one or more words in the text with a similar meaning to each word.

B Complete the summary with words from Exercise A. You may need to change the form or add extra words.

C Study the words in box b.

1 What is each base word and its legal meaning?

2 How does the affix change the part of speech?

3 What is the meaning in the text in Lesson 2?

D Study sentences A–E on the opposite page.

1 Copy and complete Table 1. Put the parts of each sentence in the correct box.

2 Rewrite the main part of each sentence, changing the verb from active to passive or vice versa.

E Look at the 'Other verbs' column in Table 1.

1 How are the clauses linked to the main part of the sentence?

2 In sentences A–C, what does the word *which* refer to?

3 Make the clauses into complete sentences.

> **a**
> trespass   intend   steal
> accused   allege   possession   commit
> fear   amount to   crime   necessary

> The Theft Act 1968 covers a number of crimes. Burglary involves _____ in a building with the intent to _____ . Aggravated burglary is committed if a person is _____ a weapon of offence at the time of the burglary. The _____ does not actually have to use it. The possession of the weapon is sufficient for the crime to _____ aggravated burglary.
>
> Finally, robbery requires the use of force before or at the time the _____ is committed. It is not _____ for force to be actually used while the person is _____ the crime. It is sufficient for a person to put another person in _____ of force.

> **b**
> burglary   aggravated
> implication   defendant   householder
> enabled   upheld   conviction

A Make one sentence for each box on the right, using the method given in red. Include the words in blue. Write all the sentences as one paragraph.

B Study the notes on the opposite page which a student made about the crime of robbery. Write up the information.

1 Divide the notes into sections to make suitable paragraphs.

2 Write a topic sentence for each paragraph.

3 Make full sentences from the notes, joining ideas where possible, to make one continuous text.

> McGill borrowed a car to drive his wife to the railway station for the Hastings train.
> A friend owned the car.
>
> relative, passive   In 1970

> He arrived at the station too late for the train.
> He used the car to drive his wife to Hastings.
>
> participle   In fact

> He did not have the owner's permission for this journey.
> He didn't return the car for three days.
>
> passive   Although

> The court convicted him.
> He was found guilty of taking the vehicle without the owner's consent.
>
> participle   As a result

A · In *R v Phipps and McGill* [1970], McGill was lent a car which he used to take his wife to the railway station.

B · Three of the crimes with which a person can be charged under the Theft Act will be described here.

C · According to the direction of the trial judge to the jury, the offence of taking without the owner's consent had been committed by McGill when he decided not to return the car at the time which was agreed.

D · As well as being a trespasser, the accused must be carrying a weapon of offence at the time of the burglary.

E · Having taken these steps as part of an illegal activity, the accused saw a huge increase in revenue.

Table 1: Breaking a complex sentence into constituent parts

	Main S	Main V	Main O/C	Other V + S/O/C	Adv. phrases
A	McGill	was lent	a car	which he used to take his wife to the railway station.	In R v Phipps and McGill [1970],
B					

Theft Act 1968 = consolidation previous Acts

covers range of crimes - all = appropriation inc.:

- TWOC
- burglary
- aggravated burglary
- robbery

definition of robbery under s.8 = use of force

- @ time
- before

but not nec. *inside* building (= aggravated burglary)

3 main elements of robbery (must exist for conviction):

- steals (s.l: steal = theft, i.e., dishonestly appropriate something with the intention of permanently depriving another person of it)
- use or threat of force (no def. in Act but = even min. physical action)
- mens rea

poss. defences inc.:

- A uses force on B but A thinks money etc. = his
- force or threat of force used after crime
- force but no theft

but 'appropriation temporary' = no defence (e.g., Corcoran v Anderton [1980] 72 Cr App R 104: A snatched handbag; it fell to the ground; A ran off without handbag. A was convicted of robbery)

case law - statutory interpretation

- R v Robinson [1977] Crim LR 173 = no theft of money (person believed he had a legal right to it)
- R v Clouden [1987] Crim LR 56 = conviction upheld on appeal (although force used to snatch handbag was minimal)

Reporting findings

You cannot use another writer's words unless you directly quote. Instead, you must restate or **paraphrase**. But be very careful with precise legal terminology. For example, *burglary* is not the same as *robbery*.

There are several useful ways to do this:

use a synonym of a word or phrase	*permission → consent* *at the hearing → in court*
change negative to positive and vice versa	*the appeal failed → the appeal did not succeed*
use a replacement subject	*the defendant may appeal → there may be an appeal against the conviction*
change from active to passive or vice versa	*the judge can direct the jury to bring in a verdict of not guilty → the jury can be directed to bring in a not guilty verdict*
change the order of information	*in the summing up, the judge outlined the facts of the case → the facts of the case were outlined during the judge's summing up*

When reporting findings from one source, you should use all the methods above.

Example:

Original text	*McGill was loaned a car for the express purpose of taking his wife to the railway station.*
Report	*The defendant borrowed a car solely in order to take his spouse to catch a train.*

Important

When paraphrasing, you should aim to make sure that 90% of the words you use are different from the original. It is not enough to change only a few vocabulary items: this will result in plagiarism.

Example:

Original text	*If convicted, the accused could be sent to prison for life.*
Plagiarism	*If the accused is convicted, he could be sent to prison for life.*

Finding the main information

Sentences in legal texts are often very long.

Example:
*Under section 1 of the Theft Act, a **person** is guilty of theft if he dishonestly **appropriates** property belonging to another with the intention of permanently depriving the other of it.*

You often don't have to understand every word, but you must **identify the subject, the verb and the object**, if there is one.

For example, in the sentence above, we find:
subject = *a person*
verb = *appropriates*
object = *property*

Remember!

You can remove any leading prepositional phrases at this point to help you find the subject, e.g., *Under section 1 of the Theft Act …*

You must then find **the main words which modify** the subject, the verb and the object or complement.

In the sentence above we find:
***Which** person?* = someone who is guilty of theft
***How** appropriates?* = dishonestly
***What** property?* = belonging to another

7.1 Vocabulary — compound nouns • fixed phrases

A Study the words in box a.

   1 Match the words in column 1 with nouns in column 2 to make phrases.

   2 Which word in each phrase has the strongest stress?

B Study the phrases in box b.

   1 Complete each phrase with one word.

   2 Is each phrase followed by:
- a noun (including gerund)?
- subject + verb?
- an infinitive?

   3 How is each phrase used?

C Read extracts A–F on the right of this page. They are from a leaflet about contracts.

   1 Read each extract carefully.

   2 Complete each extract with a phrase from box b or box c.

c
as soon as   counter-offer
genuine offer   in full
legally binding   the terms of
unqualified acceptance

D Look at the pictures on the opposite page showing possible stages in the formation of a contract.

   1 Match each picture to the correct extract (a–e) below the pictures.

   2 At which stage do you think the contract is likely to be formed?

E Read the Hadford University handout on the law and online shopping on the opposite page.

Complete the text by using one of the words in box d in each of the spaces.

d
acceptance   formation
invitation   offer

a	1	2
	appeal bank	robbery judge
	contract law	act term
	penalty prison	clause stand
	theft trial	price court
	witness	judge

b
as shown ...   as well ...   in addition ...
in order ...   in such a way ...   in the case ...
known ...   the end ...   the use ...

Formation of a contract

A A contract may be defined as an agreement between two or more parties that is intended to be _____ _____ .

B In order for a contract to exist there must be an agreement which consists of an offer and an acceptance. Two parties, at least, are needed. One of the parties, _____ _____ the offeror, is the party that makes the offer. The other, known as the offeree, is the party that accepts.

C An offer is an expression of willingness to contract made with the intention that it becomes binding on the offeror _____ _____ _____ it is accepted by the offeree.

D A _____ _____ is different from an invitation to treat. _____ _____ _____ _____ an invitation to treat, a party merely invites offers that can then be accepted or rejected.

E An acceptance is a final _____ _____ of the terms of the offer. These must be accepted _____ _____ by the offeree.

F If the offeree introduces a new term or varies _____ _____ _____ the offer then this will not be an acceptance. Instead, it is a _____ _____ that the offeror is free to accept or reject.

(a) In an auction, the auctioneer's call for bids is an invitation to treat, a request for offers. The bids made by persons at the auction are offers, which the auctioneer can accept or reject.

(b) The display of goods with a price ticket attached on a supermarket shelf is not an offer to sell but an invitation to the customers to make an offer to buy.

(c) Advertisements of goods for sale are normally interpreted as invitations to treat. However, advertisements which are open to everyone and promise a reward may be interpreted as offers.

(d) It is generally agreed that, if an acceptance is made in a letter, it comes into force from the time the letter is posted.

(e) Websites which sell products are normally treated like shop windows. Online traders should clearly state in their terms and conditions that the display of items for sale is only an invitation to treat.

HADFORD *University*

The law and online shopping

Online shopping is now a popular and convenient way to purchase goods. Choosing and paying for something you have seen on the Web can be done in a few simple steps. The stages for the _____ of a contract are basically the same as when buying goods in a shop. The display of the goods on the Web is a(n) _____ to treat. The prospective purchaser then makes a(n) _____ by clicking on the item and adding it to the shopping basket. The _____ is made when the purchaser pays by credit card or other online payment system.

A You are going to hear this lecture. Write four questions you would like answered.

B 🎧 Listen to Part 1 of the lecture.

   1 What is the lecturer going to talk about today? Write *yes* or *no*.
- the doctrine of consideration   ____
- the postal rule   ____
- the *quid pro quo*   ____
- executory contracts   ____
- executed contracts   ____

   2 What is the role of consideration in the formation of a contract?

C 🎧 Listen to Part 2 of the lecture.

   1 Make notes in an appropriate form.

   2 What is the meaning of the phrase *quid pro quo*?

   3 What four elements must be present for a contract to be formed?

   4 What promise did Thomas make to Roscorla?

   5 Why was the promise unenforceable?

   6 Were your questions in Exercise A answered?

D Match each phrase in the first column of the table on the right with the type of information that can follow.

E 🎧 Listen to Part 3 of the lecture.

   1 Makes notes on the information that comes after the phrases in Exercise D.

   2 Were your questions in Exercise A answered?

🍁 **HADFORD** *University*

Faculty: Law

Consideration under English law (Lecture 1)
- doctrine of consideration
- formation of a contract
- executory/executed contracts
- judges' interpretations of consideration

Fixed phrase	Followed by …
1 An important concept (is) …	a different way to think about the topic
2 What do I mean by …?	an imaginary example
3 As you can see, …	a key statement or idea
4 Looking at it another way, …	a general idea put into a legal context
5 In legal terms, …	a new idea or topic that the lecturer wants to discuss
6 Say …	a comment about a diagram, picture, case, example, etc.
7 The point is …	an explanation of a word or phrase

F 🎧 Listen for sentences 1–4 in Part 4 of the lecture. Which sentence (**a** or **b**) follows in each case? Why? See *Skills bank*

   1 Perhaps I should just say something about past consideration.
     a The basic rule is that past consideration is insufficient to form a contract.
     b Contracts cannot normally be formed on past consideration.

   2 One exception is the later promise.
     a If a later promise can be linked to the initial request, the consideration for the later promise can be treated as all part of one agreement.
     b Consideration for a later promise can be treated as all part of one agreement, if a later promise can be linked to the initial request.

   3 The old case of *Lampleigh* v *Braithwaite* illustrates this.
     a The case demonstrates that the court can consider later promises.
     b What this case demonstrates is that the court can consider later promises.

   4 However, Braithwaite broke his promise and did not pay Lampleigh.
     a The significance of the court's finding was extremely high.
     b What the court held was extremely significant.

7.3 Extending skills

stress within words • fixed phrases • giving sentences a special focus

A 🎧 Listen to some stressed syllables. Identify the word below in each case. Number each word.

Example:

You hear: *1 ga* /geɪ/   You write:

consideration	___	enforce	___	performance	___
contract	___	executory	___	privity	___
detriment	___	intention	___	promise	___
doctrine	___	obligation	l	sufficient	___

B 🎧 Listen to the final part of the lecture from Lesson 2 (Part 5).

1 Complete the notes on the right by adding a symbol in each space.

2 What research task(s) does the lecturer ask the students to do?

C Study the phrases from the lecture in the blue box (below right). For which of the following purposes did the lecturer use each phrase?

- to introduce a new topic
- to make a major point
- to add a point
- to finish a list
- to give an example
- to restate

> Case law on consideration _____ complex
>
> _____ number of diff. factors in any agreement _____ judges interpret diff. ways
>
> Good consideration
>
> * must be <u>sufficient</u>, i.e. measurable in economic terms
>
> * does not have to be <u>adequate</u>, _____ what offeree offers does not have to match what offerer thinks is real value
>
> Judicial interpretation _____ Chappell v Nestlé (choc. wrappers _____ good consideration)

D Rewrite these sentences to give a special focus. Begin with the words in brackets.

1 In *Chappell v Nestlé*, the judges decided that consideration need not be adequate. (*It*)

2 The case was heard in the House of Lords in 1960. (*It*)

3 The concept of consideration is very important for the formation of a contract. (*What*)

4 The concept of consideration is complex because the interpretation of what is sufficient is based on a wide variety of factors. (*The reason why*)

5 Consideration ensures that there is always a *quid pro quo* in a contract. (*The advantage*)

See *Skills bank*

> The fact of the matter is, …
> Not to mention the fact that …
> Let's take …
> et cetera
> You've probably heard of …
> In other words, …

E Choose one section of the lecture. Refer to your notes and give a spoken summary. Use the fixed phrases and ways of giving special focus that you have looked at.

See *Vocabulary bank* and *Skills bank*

A Look at the case notes on the opposite page. In each of these cases, was the judgment in favour of the plaintiff or the defendant?

B 🎧 Listen to the first extract from a seminar about the concept of good consideration.

1   What question will the students discuss?

2   Why was the decision in *Williams* v *Roffey Bros* contentious?

C 🎧 Listen to Extract 2 of the seminar. Are these sentences true or false?

1   Performance of an existing contractual duty is not consideration.

2   In *Stilk* v *Myrick*, it was held that the sailors had only fulfilled their contractual obligations.

3   Roffey Bros had to pay the additional money they had promised to Williams.

4   A promise to pay extra money is not enforceable without good consideration.

5   *Williams* v *Roffey Bros* overturned the judgment in *Stilk* v *Myrick*.

D Study tasks a–d below and the phrases in the blue box.

1   Write a, b, c or d next to each phrase to show its use.
  a   introducing
  b   asking for clarification
  c   agreeing/disagreeing
  d   clarifying

2   🎧 Listen to Extract 2 again to check your answers.

E Work in groups of four to research consideration. Each person should research a different aspect.

Student A: read about *sufficient consideration* on page 103.

Student B: read about *adequate consideration* on page 103.

Student C: read about *past consideration* on page 105.

Student D: read about *practical benefit as consideration* on page 105.

After reading the notes, report back orally to your group. Use fixed phrases to ask for and give clarification.

I'd like to make two points. First, …	____
Can you expand on that?	____
The point is …	____
What's your second point?	____
My second point is that …	____
Yes, but …	____
I don't agree with that because …	____
Sorry, but what are we talking about, exactly?	____
We need to be clear here.	____
I'd just like to say that …	____
In what way?	____
What I'm trying to say is, …	____
Can you give me an example?	____
Look at it this way.	____
Absolutely.	____

Williams v *Roffey Bros* [1991] 1 QB 1, CA

The plaintiff is a carpenter. The defendants are building contractors who in September 1985 had entered into a contract with Shepherds Bush Housing Association Ltd to renovate a block of flats. The defendants were the main contractors for these renovations. The defendants engaged the plaintiff to carry out the carpentry work in the renovation of 27 flats, including work to the structure of the roof. The plaintiff undertook to provide the labour for the carpentry work to the roof of the block and for the carpentry work required in each of the 27 flats for a total price of £20,000. By the end of March 1986 the plaintiff was in financial difficulty partly because the original contract price for the work he was doing was too low. It did not cover all the costs. The defendants were worried that the work would not be completed on time and the owners of the flats would invoke the penalty clause for late completion. The defendants agreed to pay the plaintiff an extra sum of money to ensure the work was finished on time. The defendants later refused to pay the additional sum.

Held: where the original sub-contract price is too low, and the parties subsequently agree that extra money should be paid to the subcontractor, this agreement is in the interests of both parties. The agreement therefore does not fail for lack of consideration.

Stilk v *Myrick* (1809) 2 Camp 317

On a voyage to the Baltic, two seamen ran away from the ship. The captain agreed with the rest of the crew that if they got the ship back to London without the two seamen being replaced, he would divide the money he would have paid to these two deserters between the rest of the crew. On arrival in London the captain paid the crew only the money there were entitled to under their contract. Members of the crew sued the captain for the extra money they claimed they were entitled to.

Held: the seamen's action to recover their extra pay was dismissed. The judges decided that they had only carried out their duties under the original contract and there was therefore no consideration given for the extra pay.

Recognizing fixed phrases from legal English (1)

There are many fixed phrases in the field of law.

Examples:

Phrase	Meaning in the discipline
display of goods	items available in a shop that customers can make offers to buy
competitive tender	a bid against other companies for a contract, giving information about the price and the service to be provided
invitation to treat	an invitation to open negotiations with a view to forming a contract
breach of contract	a situation where a binding agreement is not honoured by one of the parties

Keep a list of fixed phrases used in legal English and remind yourself regularly of the meaning.

Recognizing fixed phrases from academic English (1)

There are also a large number of fixed phrases which are commonly used in academic English in general.

Examples:

Phrase	What comes next?
As we have seen …	a reminder of previous information
An important concept is …	one of the basic points underlying the topic
As you can see, …	a reference to an illustration OR a logical conclusion from previous information
As shown in …	a reference to a diagram, table, case, etc.
… in such a way that …	a result of something
In addition to (X, Y)	X = reminder of last point, Y = new point
As well as (X, Y)	
In the case of …	a reference to a particular topic or, more often, sub topic
At the same time, …	an action or idea which must be considered alongside another action or idea
… based on …	a piece of research, a theory, an idea
Bear in mind (that) …	key information which helps to explain (or limit in some way) previous information
The point is …	the basic information underlying an explanation
in order to (do X, Y)	X = objective, Y = necessary actions/conditions
In financial terms, …	the cost of something previously mentioned
In other words, …	the same information put in a different way
Looking at it another way, …	
In this way …	a result from previous information
Say …	an example
What do I mean by (X)?	an explanation of X

Make sure you know what kind of information comes next.

'Given' and 'new' information in sentences

In English, we can put important information at the beginning or at the end of a sentence. There are two types of important information.

1 Information which the listener or reader already knows, from general knowledge or from previous information in the text. This can be called 'given' information. It normally goes at the beginning of the sentence.

2 Information which is new in this text. This can be called 'new' information. It normally goes at the end of a sentence.

Example:
In Lesson 2, the lecturer is talking about the doctrine of consideration in general = given information.

Given	New
One exception is	the later promise.
Perhaps the later promise	can be linked to the initial request.

Giving sentences a special focus

We sometimes change the normal word order to emphasize a particular point, e.g., a person or case, an object, a time.

Examples:

Normal sentence	Chappell v Nestlé established the rule that consideration need not be adequate.
Focusing on case	It was Chappell v Nestlé which ...
Focusing on object	It was the rule that consideration need not be adequate that was established in Chappell v Nestlé.
Focusing on time	It was in the early 1960s that Chappell v Nestlé ...

Introducing new information

We can use special structures to introduce a new topic.

Examples:
The doctrine of consideration is my subject today.
➜ *What I am going to talk about today is the doctrine of consideration.*

Consideration is very important.
➜ *What is very important is consideration.*

Money causes the problem.
➜ *The reason for the problem is money.*

Lack of consideration leads to the contract being void.
➜ *The result of lack of consideration is that the contract will be void.*

Clarifying points

When we are speaking, we often have to clarify points. There are many expressions which we can use.

Examples:
Let me put it another way ...
Look at it this way ...

What I'm trying to say is ...
The point/thing is ...

8 CONTRACT LAW 2: MISREPRESENTATION

A Discuss the following questions.

1 What do you think is meant by *misrepresentation* in contract law? (Clue: remove the affixes to find the base word.)

2 The items in box a are connected with misrepresentation. Give an example of each kind of misrepresentation.

> **a** fraudulent   innocent   negligent

> **b** onus   opinion   party   position
> redress   reliance   statement
> tenancy   term   warranty

B Look up each noun in box b in a dictionary.

1 Is it countable, uncountable or both?

2 What is its legal meaning?

3 Can you think of a synonym?

4 What useful grammatical information can you find?

c	
lease	break
sue	rescind
hold	seek
claim	comprise
breach	decide
constitute	persuade
cancel	let
induce	enter into
sign	prosecute

C Study the two lists of verbs in box c.

1 Match the verbs with similar meanings.

2 Make nouns from the verbs if possible.

D Look at the report of *Esso Petroleum Company Ltd* v *Mardon* on this page. Rewrite each sentence to make paraphrases of the text. Use:

- synonyms you have found yourself
- synonyms from Exercise B
- words from Exercise C
- passives where possible
- any other words that are necessary

Example:
Mardon was interested in leasing a petrol station.

The defendant wanted to take a tenancy on a filling station.

E Study the information on misrepresentation on the opposite page. Then read one of the cases, A, B or C, underneath the information.

1 What kind of misrepresentation was involved in the case?

2 Work in groups of three with one A, one B and one C. Give the facts of your case, in your own words. Reach a consensus on the judgment.

3 Listen to the judgments. Did you reach the same conclusions?

Esso Petroleum Company Ltd v *Mardon* [1976] QB 1, CA

Mardon was interested in leasing a petrol station. An experienced sales representative from Esso visited him and told him that sales of petrol would be 200,000 gallons in Year 3. Mardon entered into a three-year tenancy agreement for the petrol station and did all he could to promote business. However, the site was in a bad location, and Mardon sold only about 60,000 gallons in the third year. He lost money and could not pay Esso for the petrol they supplied. Esso sued Mardon for money due but Mardon claimed compensation from Esso for misrepresentation.

It was held by Lord Denning that Esso's representative had special knowledge and skill which induced Mardon to take the tenancy. The forecast of petrol sales was wrong and this constituted a breach of warranty.

Misrepresentation in a contract

False statement of fact

An actionable misrepresentation must be a false statement of fact.

The following do not therefore constitute actionable misrepresentations:

- an opinion which proves to be false
- a false statement of future intention, unless the statement forms part of the contract
- a false statement of the law

Exceptions

There are three fundamental exceptions to this rule:

1 half-truths, which are partially true statements intended to deceive or mislead
2 statements which become false
3 contracts *uberrimae fidei* which means they are made in the utmost good faith

Bisset v *Wilkinson* [1927] AC 177, HL

Bisset bought land from a farmer called Wilkinson because he wanted to farm sheep on the land. Wilkinson told Bisset: 'If you work the land properly, you could have 2,000 sheep on it.' In fact, Wilkinson had never farmed sheep on this land and Bisset knew this.

Bisset later found that the land could not support that number of animals and he sued Wilkinson for misrepresentation.

Hedley Byrne and Co Ltd v *Heller and Partners* [1964] AC 465, HL

Hedley Byrne (HB) were advertising agents. They intended to advertise for Easipower Ltd and wanted to know if the company was creditworthy. Easipower's bankers, Heller, told HB's bankers that Easipower were good for £100,000 per year for advertising. They wrote in the letter that this information was *in confidence and without responsibility on our part.*

HB relied on this statement and placed orders on Easipower's behalf. Easipower went bankrupt. HB sued Heller for damages.

Williams v *Natural Life Health Foods* [1998] UKHL 17

Natural Life Health Foods (NLHF) sold health food products through franchises. In their brochure, they offered prospective franchisees substantial income. The brochure was mainly written by Richard Mistlin, NLHF's managing director.

Williams took out a franchise but the business was not successful so he sued NLHF but it subsequently went out of business. Williams then claimed that Mistlin should be personally responsible for the losses as Mistlin had made the negligent misstatements.

A Look at the items in the blue box.

1 What type of misrepresentation might be made by a seller of each item?

2 What remedies might the purchaser have?

3 What defences does the seller have if a statement proves to be false?

B Look at the four essay types on the right.

1 What should the writer do in each type?

2 Match each essay type with one of the questions below the slide (A–D).

3 What topics should be covered in each essay question?

C Read the title of the text on the opposite page and the first sentence of each paragraph.

1 What will the text be about?

2 Choose one of the essay questions in Exercise B. Write four research questions which will help you to find information for your essay.

D Read the text.

1 Using your own words, make notes from the text on information for your essay question. Indicate where you need to do more research.

2 Work with another person who has chosen the same essay question as you. Compare your notes.

E Study the highlighted sentences in the text.

1 Underline all the subjects and their verbs.

2 Which is the main subject and verb for each sentence?

F Study the table on the right.

1 Match each word or phrase with its meaning.

2 Underline the words or phrases in the text which the writer uses to give the definitions.

See _Vocabulary bank_

> a sports car   an antique table
> a holiday home   a laptop   a motorbike
> a clothes shop   a sandwich

HADFORD *University*

There are four main essay types in law studies:

- descriptive
- analytical
- comparison
- argument

(A) What are the key differences between fraudulent misrepresentation and negligent misrepresentation?

(B) 'The law on misrepresentation does not adequately protect the purchaser of goods or services.' To what extent do you agree with this statement?

(C) Explain why *Hedley Byrne* v *Heller* [1964] is such an important test case.

(D) What are the four types of misrepresentation? What are the remedies if misrepresentation is proven in each case?

Word/phrase	Meaning
1 actionable in tort	fail to honour a contractual obligation
2 *caveat emptor*	parties are restored to the position they were in before the contract
3 plaintiff	can lead to legal action
4 rescission	money awarded by a court in compensation for a breach of contract
5 damages	parties entering into a contract should do so with great care
6 default	person who brings a civil action

Secrets and Lies

Where does the law stand?

Misrepresentation is a false statement of fact by one party which is relied on by another party when entering a contract. In order for the misrepresentation to be actionable, in other words, for a court to take action on behalf of the injured party, it must be a statement of fact. It must not be just an expression of opinion or future intention. False statements about the law are not actionable as there is a presumption that everyone knows the law. If a person remains silent about something that might be relevant to the contract, this is also not misrepresentation, provided there is no fraud. The doctrine of *caveat emptor* or 'buyer beware' applies and a party is not under a duty to voluntarily disclose problems.

There are four recognized types of misrepresentation:
- fraudulent misrepresentation
- negligent misrepresentation
- wholly innocent misrepresentation
- negligent misrepresentation under statute.

Fraudulent misrepresentation was defined by Lord Herschell in *Derry* v *Peek* (1889). He established that it is a false statement that is made firstly knowingly, or secondly without belief in its truth, or thirdly recklessly as to whether it is true or false. On this basis, if someone makes a statement honestly believing it to be true, there is no fraud. The burden of proof is on the plaintiff, the person who brings a civil action. This means that if you say a statement has been fraudulent, then you must prove it.

Negligent misrepresentation at common law involves a person making a statement with no reasonable basis for knowing whether or not it is true or false. It was first seen in *Hedley Byrne* v *Heller* [1964] where the court decided that a negligent misstatement could be actionable in tort. In other words, there might be a case even if there was no breach of contract. In *Esso Petroleum Company Ltd* v *Mardon* [1976], Lord Denning, in his inimitable way, developed this concept so that it became part of contract law. The remedy is usually an award of damages.

Wholly innocent misrepresentation differs from negligent misrepresentation in one key element. The person making a false statement has reasonable grounds for believing it to be true.

Before *Hedley Byrne* v *Heller*, the courts held that all misrepresentations that were not fraudulent were innocent. The remedy for innocent misrepresentation is usually rescission, where the parties are returned to the position they were in before the formation of the contract. Section 2(2) of the Misrepresentation Act 1967 also gives the court the discretion to award damages instead of rescission, if it is considered equitable to do so.

Negligent misrepresentation under statute is where a case is brought under the Misrepresentation Act 1967. Section 2 of the Act states that, where a person has entered into a contract as a result of misrepresentation, and has subsequently suffered a loss, then the person making the misrepresentation is liable for damages (monetary compensation), even though the misrepresentation was not made fraudulently. That person must prove that he/she had reasonable grounds to believe, and did believe, that the misrepresentation was true, up to the time the contract was made. So, under this statute, the burden shifts to the defendant, who has to prove that there were reasonable grounds to believe that the statement was made truthfully.

There seems to be some conflict between the remedies that are available under common law and those that have been brought in by statute. This conflict arises with negligent misrepresentation which is not fraudulent. Under section 2(2) of the Misrepresentation Act 1967, the courts have the discretion to award damages instead of rescission, even if there has been no fraud. However, under the common law, the rule seems to be that the courts will only allow rescission of the contract and will not award damages when the misrepresentation is not fraudulent.

In *Royscott Trust Ltd* v *Royston* [1991] a car dealer induced a finance company to enter into a credit agreement with a customer by mistakenly misrepresenting the amount of the deposit that had been paid. The customer did not make the monthly payments and later sold the car to a third party. The Court of Appeal decided that the dealer was liable for all the losses suffered by the finance company under sections 2(1) and 2(2) of the Act. It was foreseeable that a person buying a car on credit might default (that is, fail to honour their contractual obligation) and then sell the car.

A Find the words in the blue box in the text in Lesson 2.

1 What part of speech is each word?

2 Think of another word which could be used in place of the word in the text. Use your dictionary if necessary.

> false   presumption   doctrine
> beware   recklessly   remedy
> discretion   equitable   liable

B Study sentences A–D on the right.

1 Identify the dependent clause.

2 Copy the table under the sentences and write the parts of each dependent clause in the table.

3 Rewrite the sentence using an active construction.

Example:

… is where the plantiff brings a case under the Misrepresentation Act 1967.

(A) Negligent misstatement under statute is where a case is brought under the Misrepresentation Act 1967.

(B) Misrepresentation is held to be innocent when false information is not given deliberately.

(C) Fraudulent misrepresentation is a false statement that is made knowingly.

(D) The person making the misrepresentation is liable for damages, even though the misrepresentation was not made fraudulently.

C Read the essay plans and extracts on the opposite page.

1 Match each plan with an essay title in Lesson 2.

2 Which essay is each extract from?

3 Which part of the plan is each extract from?

Subject	Verb	By whom/what
a case	is brought	(by the plaintiff) under the Misrepresentation Act 1967

D Work with a partner.

1 Write another paragraph for one of the plans.

2 Exchange paragraphs with another pair. Can they identify where it comes from?

A Make complete sentences from these notes. Add words as necessary.

(A) negligent misrepresentation under statute   where case brought under Misrep. Act 1967

(B) Sec. 2   Act = where person   entered contract   as result of misrep. + suffered loss   then   person making misrep. = liable for damages even tho misrep. not made fraudulently

(C) defendant must prove   had reasonable grounds   believe   misrep. true   up to time contract made

(D) ∴ under this statute   burden proof   shifts   plaintiff ⟶ defendant   has to prove   reasonable grounds   believe   statement   made truthfully

(E) seems   conflict between remedies available under common law + those brought in by statute

(F) under sec. 2(2) of Misrep. Act 1967 courts   discretion   award damages instead of rescission   even if no fraud

(G) however   under   common law   rule seems to be   courts   only allow rescission   not award damages misrepresentation not fraudulent

B Check your sentences with the last two paragraphs of the text in Lesson 2.

C Look at the essay question on the opposite page.

1 What kind of essay is this?

2 Do some research and make an essay plan.

3 Write the essay.

See Skills bank

Essay plans

A

1. m. = false state. of fact by A relied on by B when ent. contract;
   diff. kinds =
   - f.m.
   - n.m.
   - w.i.m.
   - n.m. under stat.
2. remedies =
   - f.m. = ???
   - n.m. = rescission or damages
3. law = ✓ purchaser ∴ can sue for resc. or dam.

   BUT

   ✓ seller ∴ not have to reveal <u>all</u> facts

   caveat emptor
4. my opinion !!!

B

1. f.m. = state. know ≠ true, or don't check if true

   def. in Derry v Peek (1889)

   n.m. = state. = can't know if true or not
   1st seen in *Hedley Byrne v Heller* [1964]

2. f.m.
   - defences = ???
   - remedies = ???

3. n.m.
   - defences = ???
   - remedy = damages (usu.)

Essay extracts

1

The first type of misrepresentation in law is fraudulent misrepresentation, which occurs when you make a statement knowing it to be untrue. It can also occur when you make a statement which you do not bother to check the truth of. This type of misrepresentation was defined in the case of *Derry* v *Peek* (1889). The second type of misrepresentation, negligent misrepresentation, happens when you can't know whether a statement is true or not. This was first seen in the case of *Hedley Byrne* v *Heller* [1964]. Thirdly, there is wholly innocent misrepresentation, which, as the name implies, can happen when, quite innocently, one party makes a statement believing it to be true, although it later turns out to be false. Finally, there is negligent misrepresentation under statute, which can apply in the case of a contract entered into because of a false statement, even if that statement was not made fraudulently.

2

The case was extremely significant. The plaintiffs lost, because the court held that the disclaimer which they had written was sufficient to exempt them from a claim. However, the court also held that a special duty of care could exist between two parties, even if there was no contract. In this case, a negligent misstatement could lead to a civil claim.

Essay question

Waynesville College prepares students for university in the UK. The college states in its brochure:

All students will be placed in suitable accommodation within an hour by public transport from the college.
All classes are taught by fully qualified and highly experienced teachers.

Student X shared a room with three other students. It generally took him an hour and a half to reach the college. His teacher had only just graduated from university. Student X failed to get into university and wants to sue Waynesville College.

Advise Student X on the legal implications and possible outcomes of this case.

Understanding new words: using definitions

You will often find new words in academic and legal texts. Sometimes you will not be able to understand the text unless you look the word up in a dictionary, but often a new term will be defined or explained immediately or later in the text.

Look for these indicators:

is or *are*	*Misrepresentation is a false statement of fact …*
brackets	*damages (monetary compensation)*
or	*The doctrine of caveat emptor or buyer beware applies …*
which	*… half-truths, which are partially true statements intended to deceive or mislead …*
a comma or a dash (–) immediately after the word or phrase	*… the plaintiff, the person who brings a civil action …*
phrases such as *in other words, that is*	*In order for misrepresentation to be actionable, in other words, for a court to take action on behalf of an injured party …*

Remember!

When you write assignments, you may want to define words yourself. Learn to use the methods above to give variety to your written work.

Understanding direction verbs in essay titles

Special verbs called **direction verbs** are used in essay titles. Each direction verb indicates a type of essay. You must understand the meaning of these words so you can choose the correct writing plan.

Kind of essay	Direction verbs
Descriptive	*State … Say … Outline … Describe … Summarize … What is/are …?*
Analytical	*Analyse … Explain … Comment on … Examine … Give reasons for … Why …? How …?*
Comparison/ evaluation	*Compare (and contrast) … Distinguish between … Evaluate … What are the advantages and/or disadvantages of …?*
Argument	*Discuss … Consider … (Critically) evaluate … To what extent …? How far …?*

Choosing the correct writing plan

When you are given a written assignment, you must decide on the best writing plan before you begin to write the outline. Use key words in the essay title to help you choose – see *Vocabulary bank*.

Type of essay — content	Possible structure
Descriptive writing List **the most important points** of something: e.g., in a narrative, a list of key events in chronological order; a description of key ideas in a theory or from an article you have read. Summarize points in a logical order. Example: *What are the four types of misrepresentation? What are the remedies if misrepresentation is proven in each case?*	• introduction • point/event 1 • point/event 2 • point/event 3 • conclusion

Analytical writing
List **the important points** which **in your opinion** explain the situation.
Justify your opinion in each case.
Look behind the facts at the **how** and **why**, not just **what/who/when**.
Look for and question accepted ideas and assumptions.
Example:
Explain why Hedley Byrne and Co Ltd v Heller and Partners [1964] is such an important test case.
	• introduction
	• definitions
	• **most important point:**
	  example/evidence/reason 1
	  example/evidence/reason 2
	  etc.
	• **next point:**
	  example/evidence/reason 3
	  example/evidence/reason 4
	  etc.
	• conclusion

Comparison/evaluation Decide on and define the **aspects** to compare two subjects. You may use these aspects as the basis for paragraphing. Evaluate which aspect(s) is/are better or preferable and give reasons/criteria for your opinions. Example: *What are the key differences between fraudulent misrepresentation and negligent misrepresentation?*	• introduction • **state and define aspects** Either: • **aspect 1:** subject A v B • **aspect 2:** subject A v B Or: • **subject A:** aspect 1, 2, etc. • **subject B:** aspect 1, 2, etc. etc. conclusion/evaluation
Argument writing **Analyse** and/or **evaluate**, then give your **opinion** in a **thesis statement** at the beginning or the end. Show awareness of difficulties and disagreements by mentioning counter-arguments. **Support** your opinion with evidence. Example: *'The law on misrepresentation does not adequately protect the purchaser of goods or services.' To what extent do you agree with this statement?*	• **introduction: statement of issue** • **thesis statement giving opinion** • **define terms** • **point 1:** explain + evidence • **point 2:** explain + evidence etc. • **conclusion:** implications, etc. • **introduction: statement of issue** • **define terms** • **for:** point 1, 2, etc. • **against:** point 1, 2, etc. • **conclusion: statement of opinion**

9 EMPLOYMENT LAW

9.1 Vocabulary
fixed phrases • legal words

A Match the words to make fixed phrases.

1	unfair	permit
2	disciplinary	settlement
3	financial	union
4	job	wage
5	trade	description
6	minimum	dismissal
7	employment	procedure
8	work	tribunal

B Study the words and phrases in the blue box.

1 Add a word from the first column to each phrase in the second column.

2 Which phrase can you use to:
- agree only partly with a point
- begin talking about several points
- talk about a particular example
- introduce the first of two ideas
- introduce the second of two ideas
- focus on the point which the writer/speaker thinks is the most important
- give a reason for a point
- mention an idea
- talk about certain circumstances

C Look at the pictures on the opposite page.

1 What is each person's job with Cheapco?

2 What types of work are likely to be included in each job description?

3 Why might each person be dismissed? Would the company be justified in dismissing them in each case?

4 Match each person with the correct quote (A–F).

5 Replace the words in italics with a phrase from Exercise B.

D Read the information on this page about employment law.

1 Match the blue words in this extract with the definitions on the opposite page.

2 Use your dictionary to check words you do not know.

E Complete the table on the right.

1	2
to	... start with
the	... people think
a	on ... other hand
some	to ... extent
many	on ... one hand
this	... real question is
that	on ... grounds that
	in ... case like this
	in ... sort of situation

Employment law is important for the management of companies. For example:

- Contracts of employment and job descriptions are formal documents which companies must produce when there is a dispute.

- Your employer must have a good reason for dismissing you. You normally cannot claim unfair dismissal unless you have had one year's continuous service. Regardless of the reason for the dismissal, the employer must act fairly and follow the correct procedure.

- The potentially fair ways of dismissing an employee are for: conduct at work; capability; redundancy; retirement; statutory restriction or another substantial reason.

- A substantial reason could be something such as an unresolvable personality clash with a colleague.

- Even if you do not have one year's service your dismissal may be automatically unfair if, for example, you are sacked because you take statutory paternity leave.

Verb	Noun(s)	Adjective(s)
agree	agreement	agreeable
compromise		
dismiss		
dispute		
employ		
resolve		
restrict		
retire		
serve		
settle		

Cheapco managing director

A 'I didn't think I was being paid the minimum wage and *firstly* I asked my line manager to help me. When I got no response I contacted my trade union. The next day I was called into the office and given a week's notice.'

B 'I regret that this financial quarter has been unprofitable and we have to drastically cut our costs. *Usually*, I do all I can to keep staff, but, in the current situation, I'm afraid we will have to let some people go.'

C 'I'm 65 next week and still very fit. I enjoy my job. When the managers asked to see me I thought they wanted to give me a birthday card. They gave me my dismissal cards instead. It's a disgrace. They're always complaining of being short-staffed *but* they still kick you out when you reach a certain age.'

D 'It was only a bit of fun. The customers didn't see what we were doing. They say we should enjoy our work but they never let us. *Up to a point* I understand why the management took disciplinary action, because what we did was a bit stupid. But we certainly didn't deserve the sack.'

E 'I had only been here a week when I got pregnant – they told me I couldn't work here any more *because* I wouldn't be able to stand behind the counter all day.'

F 'At the moment our staff turnover is rather high. But *the important thing is* whether we can reduce sick leave and absenteeism over the coming year.'

---

www.hadfield.ac.uk.leg.def

Definitions

A being sacked from a job in a way that entitles an employee to seek redress from an employment tribunal

B the steps that must be taken in order to ensure that the dismissal is fair

C a formal document setting out the exact terms and conditions under which a person is employed

D a detailed list of all the duties that an employee must carry out

E the way in which an employee fulfils the duties that are required in the job

F dismissal from employment either because your employer no longer needs you or your job no longer exists

G time off work that a father is entitled to following the birth (or adoption) of his child

H the period of time spent working for a company or organization

I something that is considered to be of overwhelming importance as grounds for a fair dismissal

J where an employee is prevented from fulfilling the contract of employment, because to do so would break the law

A Study the slide on the right. What questions do you think the lecturer will answer?

B 🎧 Listen to Part 1 of the lecture.

   1 Complete the *Notes* section at the bottom of this page.

   2 What is the lecturer's story about? Why is it not given in the notes?

   3 Complete the *Summary* section.

   4 Answer the *Review* questions.

C 🎧 Create a blank Cornell diagram. Listen to Part 2 of the lecture.

   1 Complete the *Notes* section.

   2 Write some *Review* questions.

   3 Complete the *Summary* section.

   4 Were your questions in Exercise A answered?

D 🎧 Study the phrases in column 1 of the blue box. Listen to some sentences from the lecture. Which type of information in column 2 follows each phrase?

HADFORD *University*

Employment Law (Lecture 1)

- Unfair dismissal – statutory
- Wrongful dismissal – common law
- Unfair and wrongful dismissal – statutes/cases

1	2
1 Increasingly we find that …	a conclusion
2 In terms of …	information about a point the speaker will make later
3 As we shall see, …	
4 It could be argued that …	an aspect of a topic the speaker wants to focus on
5 From the point of view of …	a true statement the speaker agrees with
6 It's true to say that …	a developing trend
7 Research has shown that …	an idea the speaker may not agree with
8 So it should be clear that …	

Review   **Notes**

                     <u>Dismissal from employment</u>

Two types?   = 2 types - unfair (UD) and wrongful (WD)

Unfair = statutory   1) Unfair
                         • can be same as WD

Act = ?   • statutory = _____ 1971 (WD = _____)

Where heard?   • heard in _____ not _____

Service?   • employee > _____

                         • employer = _____

Reasons?   • reasons e.g. _____

                         Example:

                         boss = do this; not your skills ⟶ do badly ⟶ dismissed

                         you = no training, outside job descrip.

                         boss = no train. needed?

Compensation?   • compensation = fixed by _____ e.g. _____

                         • employer must act fairly and follow _____ - if not = UD

                         • even if not 12 months = unfair if e.g. _____ , etc.

Breach of contract?   • can occur without _____

Summary

9.3 Extending skills
recognizing digressions • source references

A Study the words and phrases in box a.

1 Mark the main stress in each one.

2 🎧 Listen and check your answers.

3 Which word or phrase has a different stress pattern in each group?

B Study the phrases in box b.

1 Do you think the phrases show a digression (start or end) or a relevant point? Write **D** or **R**.

2 Look at the **D** phrases. Do they start or end the digression?

C 🎧 Listen to the final part of the lecture from Lesson 2 (Part 3).

1 Take notes using the Cornell system. Leave spaces if you miss information.

2 What topic does the lecturer mention that is different from the main subject?

3 Why did he mention this topic?

4 What is the research task?

5 Compare your notes in pairs. Fill in any blank spaces.

6 Complete the *Review* and *Summary* sections.

a

1 wrongful, statute, resolve, conduct (n)
2 provision, tribunal, dismissal, damages
3 employment law, common law, breach of contract, retirement age
4 actually, generally, usually, demonstrably, crucially

b

Now, where was I?

It's the first of these points that I'm going to focus on now …

By the way, …

So to get back to the main topic …

I have a little story to tell you …

If we move on now to …

You don't need to take notes on this …

The point of that story was …

If we turn now to …

When we look at wrongful dismissal we'll find …

D 🎧 What information does the lecturer provide about sources? Listen to the extracts and complete the table below.

	Extract 1	Extract 2	Extract 3	Extract 4
Name of writer				
Title and date of source				
Location				
Type of reference				
Relevant to …?				
Introducing phrase				

E Use your notes to write 75–100 words about unfair dismissal.

F Work in groups. Study the six reasons for potentially fair dismissal in box c. Choose one reason. Read the relevant information on page 104 and then discuss these questions.

1 What must an employer show in order for the reason to be genuine and justify dismissal?

2 What defences might an employee have?

3 Where can you go to find more information?

c

conduct
capability
redundancy
retirement
statutory restriction
another substantial reason

A Group the words in the blue box according to their stress pattern.

> appeal   dishonesty   genuine   justify
> legitimate   procedure   redundancy
> redress   retirement   statutory
> substantial   summarize

B Study items A–E on this page, which relate to an employee who is frequently late for work.

  1 What does each item show?

  2 What is the relevance of each item to the issue of fair dismissal?

  3 What mistakes could an employer make in this case which might lead to a claim of unfair or wrongful dismissal?

C Work in pairs.

Student A: Think of good ways to take part in a seminar.

Student B: Think of bad ways to take part in a seminar.

D You are going to hear some students in a seminar. They have been asked to talk about *either* unfair dismissal *or* wrongful dismissal.

  1 🎧 Listen to the four extracts. Say whether each contribution and is good or poor.

  2 Give reasons for your opinion.

  3 Add some more information to the good contributions.

E Work in a group of three or four.

  1 Discuss your information for the topics in Lesson 3, Exercise F. Agree on the best explanation.

  2 Discuss how best to present this information.

  3 Present your topic to the whole class.

F Study the case of *Wise Group* v *Mitchell* on the opposite page.

  1 What verdict did the Employment Tribunal reach?

  2 On what basis did the Employment Tribunal assess the level of damages that Mitchell should be awarded as a result of her wrongful dismissal?

  3 Why was the appeal by the employer allowed by the Employment Appeal Tribunal (the higher court)?

  4 What level of damages did the Employment Appeal Tribunal decide that Mitchell should receive?

  5 Do you think the verdict in this case was fair?

A

Job description

Job title Sales administration assistant

Responsible to Sales manager

Location Cambridge

Duties and responsibilities

1. Process orders from domestic and overseas customers

2. Deal with enquiries from customers via telephone and e-mail

B

Terms and conditions of service

Section 1 Hours of the working week

Section 2 Part-time employees and fixed-term contracts

Section 3 Annual leave and public holidays

Section 4 Sickness leave

Section 5 Maternity leave

verbal warning

written warning

dismissal

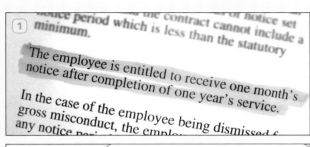

Wise Group v *Mitchell* [2003]
All ER 168; ICR 896, EAT

The claimant was sacked by her employer five weeks before she had completed one year's service. In her contract of employment, she was entitled to receive one month's notice. The employer paid her one month's salary in lieu of notice. The Employment Tribunal upheld that she had been wrongfully dismissed because the company had breached its contractual duty by not following the correct disciplinary procedures. The tribunal assessed damages on the basis that, if the company had followed the correct disciplinary procedures, she would have completed one year's continuous service which would then have entitled her to make a claim for unfair dismissal.

The employer appealed.

The Employment Appeal Tribunal held that where an employee was dismissed wrongfully for breach of contract before she had acquired the right to claim for unfair dismissal, she had no statutory right to claim unfair dismissal even if, had the correct disciplinary procedures been followed, she would have completed one year's continuous service. Damages for loss following wrongful dismissal were limited to the sums that would have been payable under the contract of employment, if the contract had been terminated lawfully. Once the dismissal had happened, it was not relevant to consider what might have happened if the disciplinary procedure had been followed correctly. Although the employer had acted unfairly in the steps taken leading up to the dismissal, that unfairness did not cause the employee any loss and there could therefore be no common law claim in respect of it.

Recognizing fixed phrases from legal English (2)

Make sure you understand these phrases from legal English.

actus reus

aggravated burglary

appeal court

assault and battery

bona fide

breach of contract

claim for damages

common law

continuous service

contract law

defamation of character

disciplinary procedure

employment law

employment tribunal

job description

judicial precedent

maternity leave

medium-neutral citation

mens rea

minimum wage

obiter dictum

paternity leave

per incuriam

persuasive authority

ratio decidendi

stare decisis

statutory invention

statutory restriction

unfair dismissal

wrongful dismissal

Recognizing fixed phrases from academic English (2)

Make sure you understand these fixed phrases from general spoken academic English.

As we shall see, …

But the real question is …

From the point of view of …

In a case like this, …

In terms of …

In the sense that …

In this sort of situation, …

That's the reason why …

Increasingly we find that …

It could be argued that …

It's true to say that …

Many people think …

On the grounds that …

On the one hand,…

Research has shown that …

So it should be clear that …

That would be great, except …

To some extent …

To start with, …

Using the Cornell note-taking system

There are many ways to take notes from a lecture. One method was developed by Walter Pauk at Cornell University, USA.

The system involves **Five Rs**.

record	Take notes during the lecture.
reduce	After the lecture turn the notes into one- or two-word questions or 'cues' which will help you remember the key information.
recite	Say the questions and answers aloud.
reflect	Decide on the best way to summarize the key information in the lecture.
review	Look again at the key words and the summary (and do this regularly).

Recognizing digressions

Lecturers sometimes move away from the main point in a lecture to tell a story or an anecdote. This is called a **digression**. You must be able to recognize the start and end of digressions in a lecture.

Sometimes a digression is directly relevant to the content of the lecture, sometimes it has some relevance and sometimes, with a poor lecturer, it may be completely irrelevant. Sometimes the lecturer points out the relevance.

Don't worry if you get lost in a digression. Just leave a space in your notes and ask people afterwards.

Recognizing the start	*That reminds me …*
	I remember once …
	By the way …
Recognizing the end	*Anyway, where was I?*
	Back to the point.
	So, as I was saying …

Understanding the relevance	*Of course, the point of that story is …*
	I'm sure you can all see that the story shows …
	Why did I tell that story? Well, …

Asking about digressions	*What was the point of the story about the legal company?*
	Why did he start talking about note-taking?
	I didn't get the bit about …

Referring to other people's ideas

We often need to talk about the ideas of other people in a lecture or a tutorial. We normally give the name of the writer and/or the name of the source. We usually introduce the reference with a phrase; we may quote directly, or we may paraphrase an idea.

Name and introducing phrase	*As Selwyn points out …*
	To quote Selwyn …
Where	*in Selwyn's Law of Employment …*
What	*we can think of unfair dismissal as …*

10 HOMICIDE

10.1 Vocabulary
'neutral' and 'marked' words • expressing confidence/tentativeness

A Study the words in box a.

  1 Use your dictionary to check the meanings.

  2 What part of speech is each word?

B Read the Hadford University handout.

  1 Use your dictionary or another source to check the meanings of the highlighted phrases.

  2 Which are the stressed syllables in each phrase? Which word in each phrase has the main stress?

C Look at the pictures on the opposite page. For each picture, talk about how you think the homicide occurred and what defence, if any, the perpetrator may have. Use some of the words from Exercise A and the highlighted phrases from Exercise B.

D Study the words in box b.

  1 Check the meanings, parts of speech and stress patterns.

  2 Put the words into the correct box in the table below, as in the example.

Neutral	Marked
hit	*batter, thump, whack*
sad	
violent	
ugly	
fall	

E Read the extract below from a law student's essay on homicide.

  1 Use marked words in place of the blue (neutral) words/phrases.

  2 Look at the red phrases. How strong are they?

> **a**   abolition   homicide   involuntary   justifiable   malice   manslaughter   murder   perpetrator   provocation   recklessly

---

HADFORD *University*

Murder

In English law, murder is considered the most serious form of homicide. For the crime of murder to be proved, the perpetrator must have intended to kill, or intended to cause serious injury where death is virtually certain to result. Following the abolition of the death penalty in 1965, the mandatory sentence for murder is life imprisonment.

There are a number of defences to a charge of murder, which can be termed mitigating circumstances. These include self-defence and provocation. There is also the defence of diminished responsibility which refers to the mental state of the accused at the time of the killing. A successful defence could lead to conviction on the lesser charge of manslaughter.

> **b**   batter   brutal   ferocious   grotesque   gruesome   heartbreaking   monstrous   plummet   plunge   savage   thump   tragic   vicious   whack

---

From the evidence in this case, it's clear that the victim was hit a number of times in a violent attack. The lady managed to escape from the attacker, but, subsequently, tripped over and fell down the stairwell to her untimely death. It's generally accepted that, if the attacker intends to cause harm, the person can be found guilty of, at the least, manslaughter. In this sad case, we undoubtedly have such a situation.

It's fair to say that the facts here fall into the category of the so-called 'escape cases'. So we could relate them to the factors laid down by Lord Keith in *DPP* v *Daley and McGhie* [1980] in the Court of Appeal. It's unlikely that a defence claim of a break in the causation between the original attack and the death of the victim would result in an acquittal, but there may be a question about whether the attacker would be convicted of murder or manslaughter.

A WOMAN WRONGED
MRS EDWARDS CONFRONTS A BURGLAR.

STRIKING MINER KILLED ON PICKET LINE
JOHN DYSON TRIES TO CROSS PICKET
LINE; LASHES OUT AFTER TAUNTS.

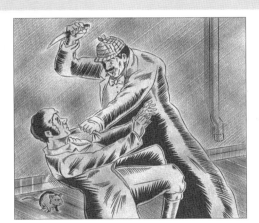

HIS STATE OF MIND WAS SO DIFFERENT FROM THAT
OF ORDINARY HUMAN BEINGS THAT THE
REASONABLE MAN WOULD TERM IT ABNORMAL.

IN DEFENCE OF KING AND COUNTRY.

OUR VALIANT UNARMED DEFENDER OF THE LAW
STOOD NO CHANCE AS THE MALICIOUS BRUTE
FIRED AT POINT-BLANK RANGE.

THE CONSEQUENCES OF RECKLESS
ACTIONS CAN BE VERY SEVERE.

A Study the sentence on the right. Each phrase in box a could go in the space. What effect would each one have on the base meaning? Mark from *** = very confident to * = very tentative.

B Survey the text on the opposite page.
  1 What will the text be about?
  2 Write three research questions.

C Read the text. Does it answer your questions?

D Answer these questions.
  1 Do the courts consider involuntary manslaughter to be a major or a minor offence?
  2 What were the relevant facts in *R v Franklin* as far as the court was concerned?
  3 What precedent did *R v Franklin* establish?
  4 What is the significance of the defendant's occupation in *R v Adomako*?
  5 In what way was the defendant in *R v Seymour* reckless?
  6 'I didn't want to kill him. I didn't even see him there!' Is this a good defence? Why (not)?

E Find the phrases in box b in the text.
  Is the writer *confident* (**C**) or *tentative* (**T**) about the information which follows?

F Read the article on the death of a train guard taken from a tabloid newspaper on page 105.
  1 Underline the marked words.
  2 What does the choice of these words tell you about the train guard widow's opinion of the way the case was handled?
  3 Find neutral words to use in their place.

G Study the example sentence on the right, and then sentences A and B.
  1 Divide sentences A and B into small parts, as in the example sentence.
  2 Underline any joining words (e.g., conjunctions).
  3 Find the subjects, verbs, objects/complements and adverbial phrases which go together.
  4 Make several short simple sentences which show the meaning.

The robbers' verbal threats and physical intimidation

_____

the heart attack which led to the death of the cashier.

a
  probably caused _____
  may have contributed to _____
  was possibly one of the factors which contributed to _____
  could have been a factor which led to
  _____
  caused _____
  seems to have caused _____

b
  It is obvious ... _____
  Many writers seem to agree ... _____
  This case appears to demonstrate ...
  _____
  many writers have claimed ... _____
  It is worth noting ... _____
  Clearly ... _____

Example:

In the English law of homicide, | manslaughter | is | a less serious offence | than murder, | with | the law | differentiating between | the levels of fault | based on | the *mens rea*.

A

Voluntary manslaughter is where the accused *intentionally* kills another, but is not liable for murder because there are mitigating circumstances such as provocation or diminished responsibility.

B

Involuntary manslaughter occurs when the accused did not *intend* to cause death or serious injury, but death resulted because that person was reckless or grossly negligent.

'Killing no murder'

Involuntary manslaughter is the term given to unlawful killing where the *mens rea* for murder is not present. It is obvious, therefore, that the defendant will not have intended to kill the victim or even to cause grievous bodily harm. How exactly do the courts view the crime?

Many writers seem to agree that there are three broad categories of involuntary manslaughter. Firstly, there is manslaughter by an unlawful or dangerous act (also known as constructive manslaughter). Secondly, we have manslaughter by gross negligence. The final category is manslaughter with subjective recklessness as to the risk of death or bodily harm. On conviction for involuntary manslaughter, the sentence is at the discretion of the judge and can range from an unconditional discharge to life imprisonment.

Let's look at the case law for each type of manslaughter. A good example of **constructive manslaughter** can be found in *R* v *Franklin* (1883), where the defendant threw into the sea 'a good-sized box' which he picked up on a pier. The box hit a swimmer and killed him. The defendant was guilty of manslaughter, as death resulted from the unlawful act of taking another's property and throwing it into the sea. This case appears to demonstrate that this type of manslaughter must involve a criminal act, which must be a 'substantial cause of death'.

In *R* v *Bateman* (1925), the Court of Appeal established that in **manslaughter by gross negligence**, there must be 'such a disregard for life and the safety of others to amount to a crime'. This was followed in *R* v *Adomako* [1995], where a hospital anaesthetist was found guilty of the manslaughter of a patient.

R v *Seymour* [1983] laid down the test for **manslaughter with subjective recklessness**. The defendant tried to push his girlfriend's car out of the way with his lorry. She was crushed between the vehicles and later died. The House of Lords defined *mens rea* for recklessness as 'an obvious and serious risk of some harm' where 'a) the defendant must have realised that risk and decided to take it or b) the defendant gave no thought to what was an obvious or serious risk of some harm.' Prior to this, there was authority that manslaughter was killing with the appropriate degree of recklessness. Card et al. (1995) refer to *Gray* v *Barr* [1971] and *R* v *Stone and Dobinson*

[1977] where the court ruled that 'indifference to an obvious risk' constituted recklessness (p. 227).

In recent years, many writers have claimed that the unlawful act must expose the victim to bodily harm, and must be aimed at the victim. Smith and Hogan (2002) refer to *R* v *Dalby* [1982]. It is worth noting that this introduces another element to the *mens rea*: it requires the defendant to direct his action against the victim. However, subsequent cases *R* v *Goodfellow* [1986], *R* v *Watson* [1989], *R* v *Mitchell* [1995] have reduced the significance of *Dalby*. According to these cases, the issue now is causation. Did one person's action directly or indirectly cause the death of another person? There is no need to show that the defendant realized the risk, only that a reasonable person in those circumstances would have realized. Clearly, if the evidence does not support the *mens rea* for the unlawful act, the defendant will not be liable.

Writers often cite the Appeal Court decision in *DPP* v *Newbury* and *DPP* v *Jones* [1977] when identifying the test for *mens rea* in involuntary manslaughter. In this case, two teenage boys threw a paving stone from a bridge that hit the guard of a train passing underneath. The guard died as a result of his injuries. The defendants were found guilty of manslaughter because they intentionally committed an unlawful and dangerous act which caused death. Whether the defendants knew that the act in question was unlawful or dangerous was not relevant.

In 2007, the Corporate Manslaughter and Corporate Homicide Act in the UK extended manslaughter to apply to organizations. This legislation followed a number of fatal accidents caused by management failures to maintain safety standards. As Alex Dobson states in an article in *The Times* (5th April 2008):

> The pressure for reform began to grow after the death of 187 people caused by the capsizing of The Herald of Free Enterprise (a cross-channel ferry) in 1987.

A detailed introduction to the Act appears on the UK Ministry of Justice website. Those interested in the background and development of the crime should read Professor Gary Slapper's article on corporate manslaughter in the *Asia-Pacific Review* (2002, pp. 161–170).

A Read the three essay questions. What types of essay are they?

B Look at text A on the opposite page. Copy and complete the first part of Table 1.

   1 Give the relevant facts of the case.

   2 Think of possible charges and defences.

   3 What do you think was the verdict?

C Look at text B on the opposite page about the case in text A. Complete the other rows of Table 1.

   1 Which charge is most likely in this case?

   2 What is the likely verdict?

D Read the title of essay 3 again.

   1 Study a plan of this essay (Resource 10D).

   2 Feed back on your research after Lesson 2.

   3 Write some notes for paragraph 3.

   4 What is the key element in evaluation of solutions in paragraph 4?

   5 Complete the essay plan.

1 Person A causes the death of Person B. What will be the charge, in the English legal system? Compare the types of homicide, using the levels of *mens rea*.

2 Explain from a legal viewpoint how the courts have interpreted involuntary manslaughter and how recent case law has changed the interpretation.

3 Describe, with some actual examples, the problems faced by the courts in establishing causation in manslaughter. Consider how the courts can best address these difficulties.

Table 1

Relevant facts of case	
Possible charges	
Possible defences	

A Expand these simple sentences. Add extra information. Use the ideas you discussed in Lesson 3.

   1 Did the action of A cause the death of B?

   2 For example, A threatens B and B dies of a heart attack.

   3 Or A threatens B and B falls down stairs and dies.

   4 The judge must guide the jury on causation.

B Copy and complete Tables 1–3. Refer to the reference list (C) on the opposite page.

C What do the abbreviations in the blue box mean?

D Look back at the text on page 81 (Lesson 2) and at text B on the opposite page.

   1 Find all the research sources (e.g., Card et al. 1995). Mark any page or paragraph numbers next to the correct reference in the list (C) on the opposite page.

   2 Find all the direct quotes in the texts. What punctuation and formatting is used before and within each direct quote? Why?

   3 What words are used to introduce each direct quote? Why does the writer choose each word?

Table 1: *Referencing books*

Author(s)	Date	Place	Publisher

Table 2: *Referencing journals*

Name of journal	Volume	Pages

Table 3: *Referencing websites*

Retrieval date	URL

&	©	cf.	edn.	ed(s).	et al.
ibid.	n.d.	op. cit.	p.	pp.	vol.

A

Manslaughter Case Study 1

A group of people went to visit a pub. During the evening, there was a disagreement between members of the group and there was some fighting and scuffling. The victim, a doorman at the pub, intervened to try to stop the fight. The pub manager asked the group to leave. They went down to their 4 x 4 vehicle in the car park. The accused got into the driving seat and three other people from the group got into the passenger seats. The victim stood in front of the car and the accused edged the car up to him and then stopped. The victim then started arguing with one of the passengers and put his head through the car window to grab him. The car was driven off with the victim halfway through the car window. As the car sped up the road, the victim's feet got caught in the front wheel and he fell on the road. He was run over and suffered severe chest injuries. He was pronounced dead two hours later.

B

It is clear that, in this case, the accused could face a murder charge, if the intention to kill could be proved. Alternatively, a charge of voluntary manslaughter could be brought if there was intent but mitigating circumstances. Finally, the prosecution could seek involuntary manslaughter by reason of unlawful or dangerous act, gross negligence or recklessness.

It is equally clear that there are possible defences against each. Firstly, it is difficult, in this case, to prove intention to kill. Secondly, the act of driving away cannot be held to be unlawful in itself, but, clearly, it could be seen as dangerous, grossly negligent or reckless under the circumstances. However, even if the driver was negligent or reckless, there may well be evidence to support defences of self-defence, duress and necessity. The judgment given by Lord Morris of Borth-y-Gest in *R* v *Palmer* [1971] AC 814, HL is quoted both in Archbold (1999) para. 19–41 and in Smith and Hogan (2002) p. 263. 'If there has been an attack so that defence is reasonably necessary, it will be recognised that the person defending himself cannot weigh to a nicety the exact measure of the defensive action.'

C

References

Archbold, J. (1999). *Archbold: Criminal Pleading, Evidence and Practice*. London: Sweet & Maxwell.

Card et al. (1995). *Card, Cross & Jones Criminal Law*. London: Butterworth.

Dobson, A. (2008). 'Corporate manslaughter: everything you need to know.' Times online, accessed 29 May 2008. Available from: http://business.timesonline.co.uk/tol/business/law/article3662674.ece.

Slapper, G. J. 'Corporate manslaughter: the changing legal scenery,' *Asia-Pacific Review* 10, 2002, pp. 161–70.

Smith, J. and Hogan, B. (2002). *Criminal Law*. Oxford: Oxford University Press.

Recognizing fixed phrases from legal English (3)

Make sure you understand these key phrases from law.

voluntary manslaughter　　　　　　*gross negligence*
involuntary manslaughter　　　　　　*malicious intent*
justifiable homicide　　　　　　　　*mandatory sentence*
self-defence　　　　　　　　　　　*diminished responsibility*

Recognizing fixed phrases from academic English (3)

Make sure you understand these key phrases from general academic English.

One of the …　　　　　　　　　　*In this sort of situation …*
In some circumstances, …　　　　　*It is obvious/clear that …*
Even so, …　　　　　　　　　　　*It appears to be the case that …*
… , as follows: …　　　　　　　　*Research has shown …*
The writers assert/conclude/suggest that …　*The evidence does not support this idea.*

Recognizing levels of confidence in research or information

In an academic context, writers will usually indicate the level of confidence in information they are giving. When you read a 'fact' in a text, look for qualifying words before it, which show the level of confidence. There is a strong tendency for writers to be tentative when stating facts.

Examples:
It appears to be the case that … / This suggests that …(**tentative**)
The evidence shows that … / It is clear that … (**definite/confident**)

Recognizing 'marked' words

Many common words in English are 'neutral', i.e., they do not imply any view on the part of the writer or speaker. However, there are often apparent synonyms which are 'marked'. They show attitude, or stance.

Examples:
*The accused **hit** the victim.* (**neutral**)
*The accused **battered** the victim.* (**marked**)

Battered implies that the writer thinks the accused used particularly strong force.

When you read a sentence, think: *Is this a neutral word, or is it a marked word? If it is marked, what does this tell me about the writer's attitude to the information?*

When you write a sentence, particularly in paraphrasing, think: *Have I used neutral words or marked words? If I have used marked words, do they show my real attitude/the attitude of the original writer?*

Extend your vocabulary by learning marked words and their exact effect.

Examples:

Neutral	Marked
sad	*tragic, appalling, heartrending*
say, state	*assert, maintain, claim, argue, allege*
take	*grab, seize, snatch*
hit	*batter, whack, thump, smack*

Identifying the parts of a long sentence

Long sentences contain many separate parts. You must be able to recognize these parts to understand the sentence as a whole. Mark up a long sentence as follows:

- Locate the subjects, verbs and objects/complements by underlining the relevant nouns, adjectives and verbs.
- Put a dividing line at the end of a phrase which begins a sentence; before a phrase at the end of the sentence; between clauses.
- Put brackets round extra pieces of information.

Example:

In some jurisdictions, a person may be found guilty of manslaughter on the basis of diminished responsibility if it can be proved that the killer was suffering from some condition such as depression or stress that affected the person's judgement at the time.

In some jurisdictions, | a person may be found guilty | of manslaughter on the basis of diminished responsibility | if it can be proved | that the killer was suffering from some condition | (such as depression or stress) | that affected the person's judgement at the time.

Constructing a long sentence

Begin with a very simple SV(O)(C)(A) sentence and then add extra information.

Example:

	Manslaughter		is	a serious offence.		
In the English law of homicide,	*manslaughter*	*both voluntary and involuntary*	*is*	*a serious offence*	*but not as serious as murder,*	*with the law differentiating between different levels of fault.*

Writing a bibliography/reference list

The Harvard system is widely used internationally in Law and other academic subjects. Information should be given as shown in the following source references for a book, a journal article and an Internet article. The final list should be in alphabetical order according to the family name of the writer. See the reference list on page 83 for a model.

Author	Date	Title of book	Place of publication	Publisher
Glazebrook, P.	(2007).	*Statutes on Criminal Law.*	Oxford:	Oxford University Press.

Writer or organization	Title of article	Journal	Reference	Date
Gobert, J.	'Searching for coherence in the law of involuntary manslaughter: The English experience,'	*Criminal Law Forum*	6,	1995.

Author	Date	Title of article	Publisher	Accessed	URL
Hencke, D.	(2007).	'Corporate manslaughter law to cover deaths in custody.'	guardian. co.uk,	8 June 2008	http://www.guardian.co.uk/politics/2007/jul/24/immigrationpolicy.prisonsandprobation

11 INTERNATIONAL LAW

11.1 Vocabulary   linking ideas

A Look at the diagram on the opposite page.

1 Study the influences on domestic law.

2 Discuss how each influence might affect the legal system of a country.

3 Give more examples of each influence.

B Study the linking words and phrases in box a.

1 Put them into two groups for:
   a discussing reasons and results
   b building an argument.

2 Is each linking word used to join ideas:
   a within a sentence?
   b between sentences?

3 Can you think of similar linking words?

4 Put the words in question 1b in a suitable order to list points in support of an argument.

C Study the words connected with international law in box b.

1 Sort the words into three groups according to whether they are nouns, verbs or adjectives.

2 What is the stress pattern of each word?

3 Can you think of other words or phrases with a similar meaning?

D Read the text on the right.

1 Complete each space with a word or phrase from box a or box b.

2 Find each word or phrase below in the text. Find later words or phrases that refer back to them, as in the example.

Example:

compulsory   *coercive*

breaches
penal system
treaties
armed conflicts
UN
power

E Do the general knowledge quiz on the opposite page.

---

a

Another point is …   As a result, because …   Finally,   Firstly,   For example, In addition,   Moreover,   One result of this is … Secondly,   since …   So …

b

agreement   body   breach   coercive compulsory   domestic   dispute   endanger interpret   monitor   punishment settlement   sovereignty   treaty   unenforceable

The Law of Nations

According to D. W. Grieg, a well-known writer on international jurisprudence, international law cannot exist in isolation from international relations. _____, international law has no established _____ judicial system for the _____ of disputes. _____, managing breaches is not as straightforward as under _____ law. Countries which _____ international law are not subject to a _____ penal system _____ there is no institutionalized _____ method. _____, there is no international police force to _____ transgressions.

_____, until the beginning of the 20th century, relations between nation states were governed by treaties. These were _____ agreements to behave in a certain way towards other states. One result of this was that countries _____ their commitments to suit their own political purposes. As the 20th century progressed, the violent armed conflicts, such as the two world wars, exposed the weaknesses of a voluntary system of international _____.

_____, in an attempt to create a stronger system of laws, the United Nations, an international law-making body, was founded. However, many scholars argue that these modern developments _____ the nation states because they take power away from state governments and cede it to international bodies. They assert that maintaining _____ is the only true international law.

Greig, D. W. (1976). *International Law*. London: Butterworth.

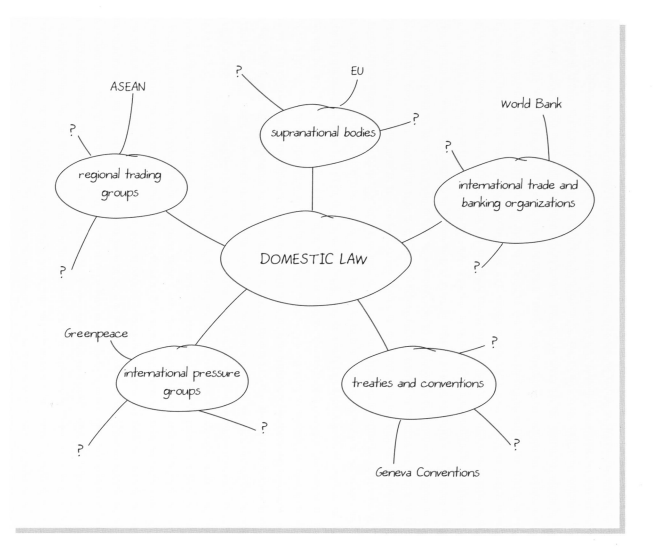

General Knowlege Quiz

1   What do these letters stand for?

   a   EU

   b   ILO

   c   ASEAN

   d   UN

   e   G8

   f   IMF

   g   WTO

   h   NAFTA

2   Who or what are these?

   a   Mercosur

   b   Kyoto Protocol

   c   Greenpeace

   d   Friends of the Earth

   e   The League of Nations

   f   Geneva Conventions

   g   Rio Declaration

   h   World Bank

A You are going to listen to a lecture by a guest speaker in the Law Faculty at Hadford University. Look at the poster on the right.

1 What is the lecture going to be about?

2 Decide on how you are going to make notes. Prepare a page for your notes.

B 🎧 Listen to Part 1 of the lecture and make notes. Then answer these questions.

1 What is the focus of the lecturer's talk?

2 What are the two types of law that the lecturer will discuss?

3 Why is she going to talk about polygamy?

4 Why does she mention Lord Denning?

C 🎧 Listen to the rest of the lecture and make notes.

D Using your notes, answer the questions on the handout on the right.

E Refer to the model Cornell notes on page 106.

1 Check your answers with the model.

2 Complete the *Review* and *Summary* sections of the Cornell notes.

F The lecturer talks about agreements on climate change.

1 Is the information fact or opinion?

2 🎧 Listen again to part of the lecture. What words tell us whether the information is fact or opinion?

G 🎧 Study the phrases in the blue box. Which type of information below follows each phrase? Listen to some sentences from the lecture.

- restatement
- definite point
- summary of a source
- an example
- statement of a topic
- another point
- tentative point
- clarification

H Write out one section of your notes in complete sentences.

HADFORD *University*

Visiting speaker: Dr Sara Smith
15th February 5.00 p.m.

'International law: *How does it affect domestic law?*'

Dr Smith will explore the way in which international law impacts on domestic law.

---

1 What influence did the lecturer discuss first?

2 What examples of this influence did the lecturer mention?

3 What is public international law concerned with?

4 Which organization:

   a helped to change laws on whaling?

   b made governments change food laws?

   c was unhappy about too many Chinese textiles coming in?

   d is a set of trading agreements?

5 What does this expression mean: 'deter defection without deterring participation'?

6 What is private international law also called?

7 Who decides in which country a case involving private citizens should be heard?

8 What is the *lex loci* rule?

---

1 that is to say

2 Don't misunderstand me, ...

3 I wouldn't go as far as ...

4 It is fair to say that ...

5 to some degree, ...

6 not only that, but ...

7 to the extent that ...

8 with respect to ...

9 ... is a case in point

10 ... has some interesting ideas

11 Briefly, (she) argues that ...

12 (She) has no doubt that ...

11.3 Extending skills
stress in phrases • building an argument

A Study the phrases in box a.

1 Mark the stressed syllables in each phrase.

2 🎧 Listen and check your answers.

3 Which phrases have adjective + noun? Which word has the stronger stress in these phrases?

B Look at the topics below.

• extradition

• universal jurisdiction

• sovereign immunity

1 What would you like to know about these topics?

2 Prepare a page to make some notes.

3 🎧 Listen to the final part of the lecture and make notes. If there is information which you miss, leave a space.

4 Compare your notes with someone else. Fill in any blank spaces.

C Answer the questions on the Hadford University handout, using your notes.

D Study the statements in box b.

1 Put the stages of building an argument (a–f) in an appropriate order.

2 Match each stage (a–f) with a phrase from box c.

E Look at box b again.

1 🎧 Listen to a section from the lecture. Make notes of what the lecturer says for each stage of the argument (a–f).

2 Check your answers to Exercises D and E1.

F Use your notes to write 75–100 words about the main points in the final part of the lecture.

G In groups, discuss the research task set by the lecturer. Talk about these questions:

1 What international agreements have addressed environmental problems?

2 Which ones will you choose to research?

3 What ideas do you have about this topic already?

---

a

alleged criminal
crimes against humanity
domestic law
extradition crimes
fugitive from justice
immunity from prosecution
international convention
judicial authorities
sovereign immunity
universal jurisdiction

 **HADFORD** *University*

1 Why did the Spanish authorities want to extradite General Pinochet to Spain?

2 What reasons did they give to justify the extradition?

3 What arguments did Pinochet's lawyers use against his extradition?

4 What decision did the House of Lords reach?

5 What is 'universal jurisdiction'?

6 What is your research task?

---

b

a giving a counter argument

b giving your opinion

c stating the issue

d supporting the reason with evidence

e rejecting a counter argument

f giving a reason for your opinion

---

c

It's quite clear to me that …

The key question is …

the facts … were not in dispute.

Some people claim …

The evidence … was compelling.

I just cannot accept …

A Study the terms in box a.

  1 Explain the meaning of the terms.

  2 Mark the main stress in each term.

B Study the words in box b.

  1 Match the words to make phrases.

  2 🎧 Listen and check your answers.

C Study the CIEL web page (A) on the opposite page.

  1 How *important* is each of its goals?

  2 How *achievable* is each of its goals?

D Study the phrases in box c.

  1 When would you use these phrases in a seminar and what for?

  2 Which phrases can you use for linking your new point to a contribution by another speaker?

E 🎧 Listen to some students taking part in a seminar; they have been asked to discuss the precautionary principle and its relevance to environmental laws. While you listen, make a note of

  1 The main topic of each extract.

  2 Further details of each topic.

F Study the CIEL web pages (A and B) and discuss these questions.

  1 What is the main message from these pages?

  2 What do you think lawyers can do to help protect the environment?

  3 Look at 'CIEL's programs' on web page A. What do you think are the aims of CIEL under each of the following headings?

    a trade and sustainable development

    b law and communities

    c biodiversity and wildlife

  Which categories in the program do you think are the most important for lawyers to do something about and why?

G Discuss your research findings on law and environmental issues with your group.

  One person from the group should report the conclusions of the discussion to the class.

---

a

climate change programme
international financial institutions
public interest movements
environmental law systems
European Union law
unified legal framework
international environment agreements
human rights abuses

---

b

Rio	Earth
Kyoto	Declaration
human	Scheme
League of	Protocol
Geneva	Union
Friends of the	Climate Change
Emissions Trading	rights
European	Nations
Intergovernmental Panel on	Conventions

---

c

I'd like to start by explaining …

To carry on from this first point, I want secondly to look at …

I don't think that is the main reason.

That seems like a very good point X is making.

I'm going to expand the topic by mentioning …

On the other hand, you might want to say that …

As well as this issue, we can also look at a very different issue.

So to sum up, we can say that …

Does anybody have any opinions or anything they would like to add?

I think we need a different viewpoint.

OK, to continue then …

Following on from what X has said …

A

The Center for International Environmental Law

The Center for International Environmental Law (CIEL) is a non-profit organization working to use international law and institutions to protect the environment, promote human health, and ensure a just and sustainable society. We provide a wide range of services including legal counsel, policy research, analysis, advocacy, education, training, and capacity building.

CIEL's goals

- To solve environmental problems and promote sustainable societies through the use of law
- To incorporate fundamental principles of ecology and justice into international law
- To strengthen national environmental law systems and support public interest movements around the world
- To educate and train public interest-minded lawyers

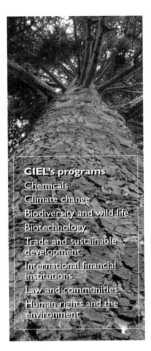

CIEL's programs
Chemicals
Climate change
Biodiversity and wild life
Biotechnology
Trade and sustainable development
International financial institutions
Law and communities
Human rights and the environment

source: www.ciel.org

B

The Center for International Environmental Law

CIEL's Climate Change Program works to develop and strengthen the rules within the international climate change regime. Although we were disappointed by the failure of the Parties to reach agreement at the Sixth Conference of the Parties (COP6) in the Hague, our primary goal remains the same: *to get the rules right* so that the Protocol can become a genuine tool for environmental protection and sustainable development.

The 4 key areas of focus for CIEL's Climate Change Program include:

1 Accounting rules that ensure verifiable emissions reductions, promote sustainable development, conserve biological diversity and respect other ecological values

2 Compliance and monitoring systems for enforcing the Kyoto Protocol

3 Participation of the public, including directly affected local communities and civil society in the Kyoto Protocol

4 Domestic policy to combat global warming

The Human Rights and Environment Program has the following goals:

- To reduce specific human rights and environmental abuses on the ground. This includes ending support for involuntary resettlement, publicizing HRE abuses and bringing "cases" to an appropriate Forum.
- To establish and promote community-based property rights in natural resources within national legal systems.
- To build the conceptual framework for using human rights in protecting the environment. This includes furthering the development of substantive human rights and sustainable development norms, and to strengthen the procedural and institutional framework for promoting HRE.
- To strengthen the human rights and environment movement through training, skill sharing, developing HRE advocacy guidelines and building strategic alliances.

source: www.ciel.org

Linking words

We use linking words and phrases to join ideas together in a sequence, to show how the ideas are related.

Some linking words can be used to join independent and dependent clauses in a sentence:

Examples:

The UK parliament is no longer sovereign **because** EU law overrides domestic law in the legal systems of member states.   OR   **Because** EU law overrides domestic law in the legal system of member states, the UK parliament is no longer sovereign.

Other linking words join sentences in a text.

Example:

EU law overrides domestic law in the legal systems of member states. **As a result**, the UK parliament is no longer sovereign.

When building an argument, it is a good idea to use linkers to add points:

Examples:

Firstly, …	Another point is …	In addition, …	… whereas …
For example, …	Secondly, …	Moreover, …	Finally, …

Using words with similar meanings to refer back in a text

It is a good idea to learn several words with similar or related meanings. We often build cohesion in a text by using different words to refer back to something previously mentioned.

Examples:

First mention	Second mention	Third mention	Fourth mention
treaty	international agreement	accord	pact
fewer …	falling numbers of …	declining …	reduced …
apply	implement	put into practice	instigate

Recognizing fixed phrases from academic English (3)

In Units 7 and 9, we learnt some key fixed phrases from general academic English. Here are some more to use when speaking:

Don't misunderstand me.	the history of …
I'm afraid that just isn't true.	the presence of …
in an attempt to …	there is a correlation between … and …
… is a case in point	to some degree …
not only that, but …	to the extent that …
Some people say …	What's more …
the effect of …	with respect to …

Writing out notes in full

When making notes we use as few words as possible. This means that when we come to write up the notes, we need to pay attention to:

- the use of numbers and symbols for words and ideas, e.g.,
  Notes: (a) conflict of laws can be seen in polygamous marriages …
  One example of conflict of laws can be seen in polygamous marriages …

- making sure the grammatical words are put back in, e.g.,
  Notes: poly. mar. legal in some countries/not in others
  Although polygamous marriage **is** legal in some countries **it is** not legal in other countries.

- making the implied meanings clear, e.g.,
  Notes: Political factors (e.g., taxation policies, pressure groups)
  Political factors **which affect business include**, for example, taxation policies, pressure groups …

Building an argument

A common way to build an argument is:

1 First, state the issue:
  Can the precautionary principle help to protect the environment?

2 Next, give a counter argument:
  Adopting the precautionary principle might slow down the economic growth in countries that can least afford it.

3 Then give your opinion:
  In fact, the precautionary principle has helped to encourage countries to put in place measures to protect the environment.

4 Then give evidence for your opinion:
  The earth summit in Rio and the Kyoto Protocol both endorsed the concept of the precautionary principle.

Linking to a previous point

When you want to move the discussion in a new direction, introduce your comments with phrases such as:
X has made some interesting points. I'd like to talk about …
Following on from what X said, I'd like to talk about …
I'm going to expand the topic by mentioning …
As well as (climate change), we can also look at a very different sort of issue.

Summarizing a source

When we talk about the ideas of other people in a lecture or a seminar, we often give a summary of the source in a sentence or two.

Examples:
A book by (name of writer) *called* (name of book) *published in* (year) *gives an explanation of how …*
Briefly, (name of writer) *explains how …*
An introduction to (topic) *can be found in* (name of writer).

12 HUMAN RIGHTS LAW

A Study the words and phrases in box a.

    1 What kind of rights would you include in each category?

    2 Read the text underneath box a. How would you group the rights in box a into Vasek's three generations?

B Read text A on the opposite page.

    1 How does the United Nations try to protect human rights?

    2 Look at the highlighted words. Connect each item to the noun it refers to.

C Study the verbs in box b. They can be used to introduce quotations or paraphrases/summaries.

    1 Check the meanings of any words you don't know.

    2 Which verbs have similar meanings?

    3 Which verbs are **not** followed by *that*?

    4 When can you use each verb?
    Example:
    accept = agree but with some reluctance; the idea is often followed by *but*

D Read text B on the opposite page. Look at the highlighted sentences.

    1 What is the purpose of each sentence?
    Example:
    Human rights are both inspirational and practical = personal belief

    2 In an assignment, should you refer to the highlighted sentences by **quoting directly** or **paraphrasing**?

    3 Choose an appropriate introductory verb from box b and write out each sentence as a direct quotation or a paraphrase. Add the source references.

E Look at the newspaper headlines on the opposite page.

    1 What abuse(s) of human rights does each headline refer to?

    2 Does the UN have a role in any/some/all of the cases?

    3 What arguments are there for the United Nations *not* acting in some/all of the cases?

F Write a short article as follows:

    What should the United Nations do to uphold human rights in member countries?

    Use information from this lesson.

---

a

citizenship   collective rights
copyright
freedom from discrimination
freedom of speech
freedom of thought
the right to a fair trial
the right to education
the right to natural resources
the right to social security

The Czech jurist Karel Vasek proposed the idea of three levels or *generations* of human rights (see *Human Rights: A Thirty-Year Struggle*, UNESCO 1977). The tripartite division relates to the three-word slogan of the French Revolution: *Liberty, Equality, Fraternity*.

First generation rights are connected with personal freedom and include the right to a fair trial, and the right to vote for your government. They are covered in Articles 3 to 21 of the Universal Declaration of Human Rights (1948) and in the International Covenant on Civil and Political Rights (1976).

Second generation rights relate to the position of an individual in society. They include the right to payments from the government if you become unemployed, or sick. They appear as Articles 22 to 27 of the Universal Declaration and in the International Covenant on Economic, Social and Cultural Rights (1976).

Third generation rights are sometimes said to be part of 'soft law', in that many of the rights do not appear in legally binding agreements. They are acknowledged in documents such as the Stockholm Declaration (1972) and the Rio Declaration on Environment and Development (1992).

---

b

accept   agree   argue   believe
cite   claim   concede   consider
contend   describe   disagree   dispute
emphasize   illustrate   indicate
insist   note   observe   point out
report   show   state   suggest

A The United Nations

The United Nations (UN) has created a global structure for protecting human rights. This is based on its Charter and on a variety of other non-binding declarations and legally binding treaties. The organization often finds it necessary to define rights in a cautious manner, as it is host to an extremely diverse group of member states, who have varying economic, social, cultural and political histories. Subsequently, the UN must find ways to accommodate such differences in its mechanisms for protecting the human rights which have been outlined in treaties and declarations. Thus, these methods may be less substantive or lack in strict enforcement as compared to those of regional institutions.

From *Study Guide – The United Nations Human Rights System* (2007) www.hrea.org/

B

page 19

Human Rights

[a]Human rights are both inspirational and practical. Human rights principles hold up the vision of a free, just, and peaceful world and set minimum standards for how individuals and institutions everywhere should treat people. [b]Human rights should also empower people with a framework for action when those minimum standards are not met. [c]Clearly, people still have human rights even if the laws or those in power do not recognize or protect them. On the other hand, people exercise human rights often without realising it. [d]As Pam Costain, a human rights activist who has worked in Central and South America, points out: 'We experience our human rights every day in the United States when we worship according to our belief, or choose not to worship at all; when we debate and criticize government policies; when we join a trade union; when we travel to other parts of the country or overseas.'*

* Costain, P. (1977). 'Moving the Agenda Forward,' *Connection to the Americas* 14, p. 4.

From Flowers, N. (ed.). (1998). *Human Rights Here and Now: Celebrating the Universal Declaration of Human Rights.* Minnesota: University of Minnesota Human Rights Centre.

RULER CRACKS DOWN ON TRADE UNIONS

Film companies aim to curb international piracy of DVDs

Army moves in to stop demonstrations

BORDER CLOSED AFTER REFUGEES FLOOD IN

Extradition sought for 'terrorist'

Military leaders turn down calls for early elections

Equal pay for equal work says women's group

A Discuss the following questions.

1 Why should countries ratify UN treaties?

2 How can the UN ensure that a country complies with the provisions of a treaty after it has been ratified?

B Survey the text on the opposite page. What will the text be about? Write three questions to which you would like answers.

C Read the text. Does it answer your questions?

D Write down three reasons why Browning believes the US government:

a did not ratify the Convention on the Rights of the Child

b should give its final approval to the CRC

E For each paragraph:

1 Identify the topic sentence.

2 Think of a suitable title.

F Look at the underlined words in the text. What do they refer back to?

G Study the highlighted words and phrases.

1 What do they have in common?

2 What linking words or phrases can you use to show:
   - addition?
   - contrast?
   - concession?
   - result?
   - reason?

3 Write the sentences with the highlighted items again, using other linking words with similar meanings.

H Read the text on the right. A student has written about the US government's reluctance to give final approval to the CRC, but the quotations and paraphrases have not been correctly done. Can you spot the mistakes and correct them?

I Write a paragraph for a university lecturer, summarizing the arguments for and against the US ratifying the CRC.

As Browning (2006) explains that although the United States helped write the UN Convention on the Rights of the Child, it was the only member of the UN, apart from Somalia, not to ratify this treaty. He argues that the United States should ratify the Convention based on an interpretation of the Convention in light of the meaning of statements about family and children in the earlier Universal Declaration of Human Rights. However, he also makes the point that arguments by the US for not ratifying the treaty become 'reasons to *pause and reflect*'. According to Browning, he says UHDR statements regarding families and children that 'made in the UDHR still, for the most part, hold in the CRC.'

THE UNITED NATIONS CONVENTION ON THE RIGHTS OF THE CHILD: SHOULD IT BE RATIFIED AND WHY?

Don S. Browning

The United States helped write the United Nations Convention on the Rights of the Child (CRC or "Convention") and signed it in 1989. But the U.S. Senate has never ratified <u>it</u>. Those who argue that the Senate should ratify the Convention point out, with both derision and glee that, along with Somalia, the United States is the only other member of the United Nations that has not officially agreed to <u>this</u> document supporting the rights of children – the most vulnerable members of the human family. Why has the United States refused to give <u>its</u> final approval? Does <u>its</u> reluctance have any justification?

This essay argues that the United States should ratify the Convention. However, the reasons advanced for <u>its</u> failure to do <u>so</u> should also be taken seriously. In the end, I conclude that the reasons do not, in reality, hold. Nonetheless, <u>that</u> conclusion is based on an interpretation of the Convention in light of the meaning of statements about family and children in the earlier Universal Declaration of Human Rights (UDHR) and other U.N. covenants that the UDHR has influenced.

Insofar as the direction of the many U.N. statements on human rights may be drifting away from the rationales of the UDHR, the grounds for refusing to ratify the Convention become reasons to pause and reflect. Upon further examination of the CRC, it is my judgment that the original meaning of statements about children and family made in the UDHR still, for the most part, hold in the CRC. For <u>this</u> reason, the Convention is safe to adopt for the United States. Furthermore, once adopted and properly interpreted, the United States could play a significant role in shaping the proper understanding and implementation of the Convention both at home and in other parts of the world.

Various groups in American society have expressed fears about the Convention and have been successful in influencing the deliberations of Senate committees contemplating <u>its</u> ratification. Groups that reject the CRC tend to be fearful that government is undermining the rights of parents over their children. <u>They</u> also tend to be skeptical of the directions of international family law and distrustful of how international treaties might trump democratic deliberations about children and families in our own individual state legislatures and courts.

Those supporting ratification of the Convention assure that the opposition's fears have no bases in reality. Supporters point to the U.S. Senate's reluctance to invoke the Supremacy Clause in implementing human rights treaties at the national level. Proponents also point to the relatively frail report-and-consultation powers of the Committee on the Rights of the Child, the only implementation body provided for by the CRC. In short, proponents insist that the Child's Rights Committee has no teeth – no powers short of embarrassment and persuasion <u>which</u> States Parties can easily ignore.

Extracts from Browning, D. 'The United Nations Convention on the Rights of the Child: Should it be ratified and why?' *Emory International Law Review* 20, 2006, pp. 157–84.

A Study the words in the box.

1 Check the pronunciation and grammar.

2 What are their meanings in a research report?

> conduct   data   discussion   findings
> implication   interview   interviewee   interviewer
> limitation   method   questionnaire   random
> recommendation   research question   respondent
> results   sample   survey   undertake

B Read the two *Method* paragraphs on the right.

1 Copy them into your notebook. Put the verbs in brackets in the correct form.

2 Identify the original research questions, the research methods and other important information.

C What are the sections of a research report? What order should they go in?

D Read the *Introduction* and *Conclusion* to Report A on the opposite page.

1 Why was the report undertaken?

2 What action(s) does the report recommend?

3 What are the elements of a good introduction and conclusion?

Report A: Method

A written questionnaire (*design*) to find out perceptions of equal opportunities (EO) and diversity among staff working in Hadford University, and the way EO policies (*see*) in relation to the types of work (*undertake*) within the university. A thousand questionnaires (*send*) to a random sample of members of staff at Hadford University, of which 150 (*return*). In addition, 130 people (*interview*) while in the workplace during one day in June.

Report B: Method

In order to find out differences between HE institutions in terms of equal opportunities policy (EOP), a review of EOPs as they appear on the Internet in six institutions (*undertake*) during the first week in June. The institutions that (*investigate*) included new, redbrick and college-based universities.

A Describe the data in Figures 1 and 2 on the opposite page. The figures are from the report into EO policies at Hadford University.

B Look at the paragraph on the right from the *Findings* section of the report .

1 Complete the spaces with quantity phrases. Put the verbs in brackets in the correct tense.

2 Write another paragraph, using Figure 2.

C Look at the notes for the *Discussion* part of the report on the opposite page. Write the discussion paragraph.

D Cover the *Conclusion* section on the opposite page.

1 What should the report writer say in the *Conclusion*? Make some notes.

2 Read the *Conclusion* again and compare.

Findings

Firstly, on the negative side, only _____ (27%) of the members of staff (*feel*) that the university's equal opportunities policy (*definitely protect*) them in the event of a problem. However, _____ of the respondents (48%) (*rate*) EOP as protecting them to some extent. A _____ (5%) (*think*) that the EOP (*not protect*) them at all. A _____ (20%) stated they (*never inform*) about the EOP. _____ (52%) of the staff who (*claim*) not to know about EOP were hourly-paid technical and manual staff. Finally, _____ (18%) of respondents (*add*) the comment that the university's EOP did not comply with current legislation.

Report A: Introduction

For a long time, equal opportunities in the workplace has been an important concept in human rights legislation. Recent legislation in the field of employment, particularly from the European Union, means that it is even more necessary now for organizations in all fields to check their equal opportunities policies. This report will describe a survey undertaken to find out the attitudes of members of staff towards equal opportunities. Recommendations will also be made as to how the institution can improve its equal opportunities policies.

Report B: Conclusion

To conclude, it is clear that there are some strengths and some weaknesses in the equal opportunities policy of the university. The university can be pleased with the high percentage of staff who feel that the EOP protects them to some extent. However, in our opinion, the institution needs to go much further in this area. First, the university should set up a small task force to review its current EO policies to ensure that they are fully in line with recent employment legislation. The task force should then recommend ways in which all staff can be informed of EO polices, especially hourly paid technical and manual staff. Finally, it should ensure that all staff have access to EO training. Unless action is taken urgently, the institution may be in danger of not fully complying with EO legislation.

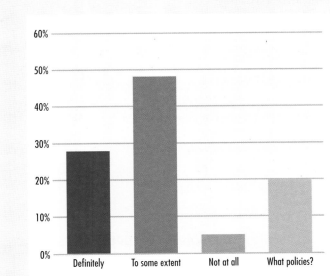

Figure 1: *Would the university's EO policies protect you?*

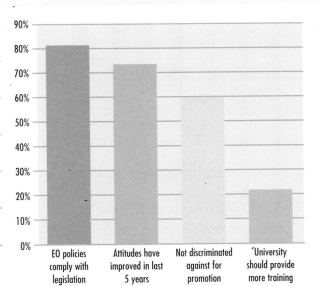

Figure 2: *How do you feel about EO at the university?*

Discussion:

Overall: EOP = relatively successful

1. 75% = protect def. / to some ext.

2. 60% = not disc. for promo.

BUT

1. 20% = what EOP?

    most = hourly paid tech. or manual = most likely to <u>benefit</u> from EOP

2. 18% = EOP <u>not</u> comply with legislation.

NB: Limitation of study: 150 respondents from 1000 quest. = 15%

Introductory verbs

Choosing the right introductory verb is important. Your choice of introductory verb shows what kind of statement the writer is making.

Example:

Browning (2006) argues that the United States should sign the UN Convention on the Rights of the Child.

Your choice of introductory verb also shows what you think of another writer's ideas. This is an important part of academic work.

Example:

Costain (1997) points out that people in the United States usually take their human rights for granted.

Verb	The writer ...
agree	thinks this idea from someone else is true
accept, concede	reluctantly thinks this idea from someone else is true
consider, emphasize, note, observe, point out, state, suggest*	is giving his/her opinion
argue, assert, claim, contend, insist	is giving an opinion that others may not agree with
cite	is referring to someone else's ideas
disagree, dispute	thinks an idea is wrong
suggest*	is giving his/her recommendation
describe	is giving a definition/description
illustrate, indicate, show	is explaining, possibly with an example
report	is giving research findings

*suggest can have two meanings

Linking ideas in a text

Linking words, which join ideas within a sentence or between sentences, convey different meanings:

	Within sentences	Between sentences
Contrast	*but, whereas, while*	*However, In/By contrast, On the other hand*
Concession	*although, despite/ in spite of the fact that*	*However, At the same time, Nevertheless, Despite/In spite of + noun, Yet*
Result	*so, so that*	*So, As a result, Consequently, Therefore*
Reason	*because, since, as*	*Because of + noun, Owing to + noun, Due to + noun*

Referring to quantities and group sizes in a report

A/An	*overwhelming/large/significant slight/small/insignificant/tiny*	majority	(of + noun)
		minority	
		number	
Over		half	
More	than	a quarter a third	
Less		x %	

Structuring a research report

A research report is an account of some research which has been undertaken to find out about a situation or a phenomenon, e.g., *What do members of staff think of our equal opportunities provisions?*

- Introduction   introduce topic; background information; reasons for research
- Methods   research questions; how research was carried out
- Findings/results   answers to research questions
- Discussion   issues arising from findings; limitations of research
- Conclusion   summary of main findings; implications; recommendations; possibilities for further research

Writing introductions and conclusions

Introduction

- Introduce the topic of the report.
- Say why the topic is important.
- Give background information.
- Give an outline of the report plan.

Note: No substantial information; this belongs in the body of the report.

Conclusion

- Summarize the main points in the report without repeating unnecessarily.
- Make some concluding comments such as likely implications or recommendations.

Note: No new information; all the main points should be in the body of the report.

Deciding when to quote and when to paraphrase

When referring to sources, you will need to decide whether to quote directly or to paraphrase/summarize.

- **Quote** when the writer's words are special or show a particularly clever use of language. This is often the case with strongly stated *definitions* or *opinions.*
- **Paraphrase/summarize** descriptions and factual information.

Incorporating quotations

- Use an introductory verb.
- Don't forget the quotation marks.
- Make the quote fit the grammar of the sentence.
- Show any missing words with '...'.

- Copy the original words exactly.
- Add emphasis with italics and write '[emphasis added]'.
- Add words which are not in the original but are necessary to fully understand the quotation out of context. Put the extra word(s) in brackets.

Do not quote more than one sentence **within the body** of a paragraph.

If you want to quote two or three sentences, put a colon and write the quote as indented text, so that it clearly stands out from the body of your essay.

However, think very carefully before you include a long quote. It is usually better to paraphrase in this case.

Additional material

5.3 Symbols and abbreviations for notes

Symbols

&, +	and, plus	↑	rises, increases, grows
–	less, minus	↓	falls, decreases, declines
±	plus or minus	"	ditto (repeats text immediately above)
=	is, equals, is the same as	∴	therefore, so
≈	is approximately equivalent to	∵	because, as, since
≠	is not, is not the same as, doesn't mean, does not equal, is different from	@	at
		C	century, as in 20th C
>	is greater than, is more than, is over	§	paragraph
<	is less than	#	number, as in #1
→	gives, produces, leads to, results in	?	this is doubtful
←	is given by, is produced by, results from, comes from		

Abbreviations

e.g.	for example	ibid.	in the same place in the source already mentioned
c.	approximately, as in c.1900	NB	important
cf.	compare	n.d.	no date given
Ch.	chapter	No., no.	number
ed./eds.	editor(s)	op. cit.	in the source already mentioned
et al.	and the other people (used when referring to a book with more than two authors)	p.	page
		pp.	pages, as in pp.1–10
etc.	and all the rest	re.	concerning
ff.	and the following, as in p.10ff.	ref.	with reference to
fig.	figure (used when giving a title to a drawing or table)	viz.	namely
		vol.	volume
i.e.	that is, that means, in other words		

Abbreviations in law

UKHL	United Kingdom House of Lords	s	section
CA	Court of Appeal	ss	sections
EWHC	England and Wales High Court	All ER	All England Law Reports
Crim	Criminal	EC	European Cases
Ch	Chancery	WLR	Weekly Law Reports
Fam	Family	CLJ	Cambridge Law Journal
R	Regina (the Crown)	BAILII	British and Irish Legal Information Institute
v	versus (against)		

7.4
Student A

Sufficient consideration

In order for the consideration to be good enough to provide the basis for the formation of a contract it must be *sufficient*. This means that it must have some economic value, even if that economic value is minimal. If a person promises not to complain about something in return for some financial benefit, this promise has no economic value and is therefore not sufficient consideration.

This was decided in the case of *White* v *Bluett* (1853) 23 LJ where it was held that a promise by a son that he would stop complaining that he was being treated differently to his other siblings in return for his father releasing him from payment of a debt was not sufficient consideration and there was therefore no contract. Pollock CB stated that: 'In reality there is no consideration. The son has no right to complain as the father can do what he liked with the money and the son abstaining from doing something he had no right to do is no consideration.'

7.4
Student B

Adequate consideration

Although consideration has to have an economic value, it does not have to be *adequate*. In other words, the consideration does not have to represent the realistic economic worth of what is given in return.

In *Midland Bank* v *Green* [1981] AC 513 the husband conveyed a farm to his wife for £500 even though the property was worth more than £40,000 in order to prevent his son from acquiring title to the property, following a family dispute. The House of Lords held that the wife was the purchaser under section 4(6) of the Land Charges Act and refused to imply into the section that the purchaser must provide valuable consideration.

9.3 Research resources – fair/unfair dismissal

Under section 94(1) of the Employment Rights Act 1996:

An employee has the right not to be unfairly dismissed by his employer.

Section 98 of the Act lists the criteria to be used in determining whether the dismissal is fair or unfair. It is for the employer to show that the reason for dismissal is justified. The categories that justify fair dismissal relate to:

- the capability or qualifications of the employee for performing work of the kind which he was employed by the employer to do. 2 (a). Under section 98(3) capability is assessed by reference to skill, aptitude, health or any other physical or mental quality and qualifications means any degree, diploma or other academic, technical or professional qualification relevant to the position which he held.
- the conduct of the employee 2 (b)
- the employee was redundant 2 (c)
- contravention of a duty or restriction imposed by or under an enactment 2 (d); this is often called statutory restriction

Under section 98(1) (b) the employer can also show 'some other substantial reason' to justify the dismissal of an employee.

The Act lists other circumstances in which an employee is unfairly dismissed.

- She is pregnant. (section 99)
- An employee brings to the attention of the employer matters which might break health and safety rules. (section 100)

In the case law, the Employment Tribunal has held that an employer can fairly dismiss employees who:

- exaggerate their academic qualifications (capability)
- steal goods or equipment from the company (conduct)
- break the law in a way which directly interferes with how they do their jobs (statutory restriction)
- make unsubstantiated accusations about members of staff (some other substantial reason)
- do not accept reasonable changes to their working conditions (some other substantial reason)

Dismissal is also fair if:

- the company no longer has suitable work to give to the employee and has acted reasonably to provide alternative types of employment within the organization (redundancy)

However, the Tribunal has found that dismissal is not fair where an employee:

- has taken time off work to look after a sick child
- has informed an exam board that the pupils in the school where he was teaching had been encouraged to cheat in their exams

References:

Employment Rights Act 1996
   www.opsi.gov.uk/acts

Employment Appeals Tribunal (EAT)
   www.employmentappeals.gov.uk

SPINELESS COWARDS

The devastated widow of the train guard branded the two youths found guilty of causing her husband's tragic death 'spineless cowards' as they were bundled into a prison van to start their sentences for manslaughter. Philomena Scott added that the two-year jail term they were each given was ludicrous and pathetic. She accused the defence of fluffing up the evidence in order to obtain a shorter sentence. The two youths claimed they were merely taking part in a prank which 'got out of hand'. They hurled massive slabs of concrete onto a railway line from a bridge when a train was passing underneath. One of the concrete slabs smacked into John Scott's head when he was working in the guard's van. He was killed instantaneously. The judge accepted that the boys did not intend to cause Mr Scott's death but their actions were unlawful and reckless. They had however shown considerable remorse about what they had done. Mrs Scott described the judge as a 'complete imbecile' and vowed that she would campaign as long as it took to get justice for her husband.

7.4
Student C

Past consideration

Past consideration is consideration that was already provided before the promise was ever made. In a bilateral contract, the consideration must be *executory* or *executed*. Executory consideration is where at the time the promises are made no performance of the contract has been undertaken, but the parties are legally obliged to carry out the terms of the contract. Executed consideration occurs in a unilateral contract where the promise is in exchange for a performed act. The case of *Stilk* v *Myrick* (1809) 2 Camp 317 provides a good illustration of where consideration has already been provided before the promise was made. The sailors had already agreed to work on the ship before the captain promised them extra money to sail the ship back to port. In *Roscorla* v *Thomas* (1842) 3 QB 234 the promise that the horse was 'sound' had been made after the horse had been sold.

7.4
Student D

Practical benefit as consideration

In some circumstances the court will accept that what appears to be past consideration can create a binding contract if it provides some practical benefit.

In *Williams* v *Roffey Bros* [1991] 1 QB 1, CA the court held that the performance of an existing contractual obligation can be taken as consideration where there is some practical benefit to the other party. In this case the builders carried out their existing contractual duty and as a result prevented the implementation of a penalty clause. The court held that avoiding having to pay the penalty clause was a practical benefit. However, the case is contentious and the courts have not always followed this ruling. In *R* v *Selectmove Ltd* [1994] BCC 349 the Inland Revenue (UK tax office) wanted to wind up a company for non-payment of debts. The company offered to pay the debts in instalments and the Inland Revenue at first agreed but subsequently went back on its promise. The court held that the company had offered no consideration in return and so the Inland Revenue was entitled to break this promise.

11.2 Model Cornell notes

Review	Notes
	Public international law = relationship between sovereign nations
	Development: (custom)/conventions → int'l orgs (e.g., ILO) → League of Nations → UN + int'l agreements (e.g., Geneva Conv.)
	Influences on pub. int'l law
	(a) Pressure groups, e.g., Greenpeace: environmental issues Friends of the Earth: also environment; tries to control big businesses (e.g., Tesco)
	(b) Regional trade organizations, e.g., EU, Mercosur, ASEAN: internal markets + protect members from competition (int'l trading agreements) e.g., in 2005 Chinese textile imports into the EU → clothes locked up until agreement reached ∴ fear for European jobs
	(c) Other organizations/agreements signed up to by governments, e.g., World Bank World Trade Organization → the rules of trade between countries
	Private international law ('conflict of laws') = disputes involving private citizens
	Plaintiff petitions, court decides whether has jurisdiction to hear case e.g., polygamous marriage? Validity in countries that do not recognize poly. mar.

Summary

List of cases

Below is a list of cases that appear in this book, with full citations.

Unit 2

Thornton v Shoe Lane Parking [1971] 1 All ER 686, CA

Young v Bristol Aeroplane Co Ltd [1944] KB 718, CA

Central London Property Trust Ltd v High Trees House Ltd [1947] KB 130

R v Taylor [1950] 2 KB 368

R v Powell (Anthony) and English [1999] 1 AC 1, HL

Miller v Jackson [1977] QB 966, CA

Spartan Steel and Alloys Ltd v Martin and Co [1972] 3 All ER 557, CA

Unit 3

J Lyons and Sons v Wilkins [1899] 1 Ch 298

Thomas v NUM [1985] 2 WLR 1081

Tuberville v Savage (1669) 86 ER 684

Wiffin v Kincard (1807) 2 Bos & PNR 471

Letang v Cooper [1964] 2 All ER 929, CA

Wilson v Pringle [1986] 2 All ER 440

Wilkinson v Downton [1897] 2 QB 57

Robinson v Balmain New Ferry [1910] AC 295

Murray v Ministry of Defence [1988] 2 All ER 521, HL

Attorney-General v BBC [1980] 3 All ER 161

Unit 4

Grobbelaar v News Group Ltd [2001] EWCA Civ 1213

Johnson (A.P.) v Unisys Ltd [2001] UKHL 13

Unit 5

R v Hinks [2000] UKHL 53

R v Gomez [1993] AC 442, HL

R v Lawrence [1972] AC 626, HL

Oxford v Moss [1979] Crim LR 119

Unit 6

R v Pearce [1973] Crim LR 321

R v Bogacki and others 1973] 2 All ER 864

R v Bow [1977] Crim LR 176

R v Stokes [1982] Crim LR 695

R v Phipps and McGill [1970] RTR 209, CA

R v Stones [1989] 1 WLR 156

R v Kelly [1996] 1 Cr App R, CA Crim

R v Dawson [1976] Crim LR 692; Cr App R 170

Corcoran v Anderton [1980] 72 Cr App R 104

R v Robinson [1977] Crim LR 173

R v Clouden [1987] Crim LR 56

Unit 7

Chappell and Co Ltd v Nestlé Co Ltd [1960] AC 87, HL

Dunlop Pneumatic Tyre Co v Selfridge [1915] AC 847, HL

Carlill v Carbolic Smoke Ball Company [1893] 1 QB 256, CA

Williams v Roffey Bros [1991] 1 QB 1, CA

Stilk v Myrick (1809) 2 Camp 317

Lampleigh v Braithwaite/Braithwait (1615) Hob 105

Roscorla v Thomas (1842) 3 QB 234

White v Bluett (1853) 23 LJ

Midland Bank v Green [1981] AC 513

R v Selectmove Ltd [1994] BCC 349

Unit 8

Esso Petroleum Company Ltd v Mardon [1976] QB 1, CA

Bisset v Wilkinson [1927] AC 177, HL

Hedley Byrne and Co Ltd v Heller and Partners [1964] AC 465, HL

Williams v Natural Life Health Foods [1998] UKHL 17

Derry v Peek (1889) All ER 1; 14 App Cas 337, HL

Unit 9

Wise Group v Mitchell [2003] All ER 168; ICR 896, EAT

Gunton v Richmond-upon-Thames [1980] ICR 755, CA

Boyo v Lambeth Borough Council [1994] ICR 727, CA

Unit 10

R v Adomako [1995] 1 AC 171

R v Franklin (1883) 15 Cox CC 163

R v Bateman (1925) 19 Cr App R 8, CCA

R v Seymour [1983] RTR 202, Cr App R 211

Gray and another v Barr (Prudential Assurance Co Ltd, third party) [1971] 2 QB 554

R v Stone and Dobinson [1977] 1 QB 354

R v Dalby [1982] 1 All ER 916, CA

R v Mitchell [1995] Crim LR 506

R v *Goodfellow* [1986] 83 Cr App R 23

R v *Watson* [1989] Crim LR 783

DPP v *Newbury*; *DPP* v *Jones* [1977] AC 500, HL

R v *Palmer* [1971] AC 814, HL

DPP v *Daley and McGhie* [1980] AC 237, HL

R v *White* [1910] 2 KB 124

R v *Malcherek*, *R* v *Steel* [1981] 2 All ER 422

R v *Pagett* [1983] 76 Cr App R 279

Unit 11

Pinochet, Re [1999] UKHL 52

Unit 12

Demjanjuk v *Petrovsky* [1985] 776 F.2d 571, United States Court of Appeals, Sixth Circuit

---

Key

All ER = All England Law Reports

KB = King's Bench

AC = Law Reports, Appeal Cases

HL = House of Lords

QB = Queen's Bench

CA = Court of Appeal

WLR = Weekly Law Reports

EWCA Civ = England and Wales Court of Appeal (Civil Division)

UKHL = United Kingdom House of Lords

Crim LR = Criminal Law Reports

RTR = Road Traffic Reports

Cr App R = Criminal Appeal Reports

Camp = Campbell's Nisi Prius Cases

Hob = Hobart's King's Bench Reports

Ch = Law Reports, Chancery Division

ICR = Industrial Cases Reports

EAT = Employment Appeals Tribunal

Cox CC = Cox's Criminal Cases

F.2d = Federal Reporter, second series

Source: Cardiff Index to Legal Abbreviations
www.legabbrevs.cardiff.ac.uk

Wordlist

Note: Where a word has more than one part of speech, this is indicated in brackets. The part of speech given is that of the word as it is used in the unit. So, for example, *assault* is listed as *assault (n)*, although it can also be a verb.

	Unit
A	
abolition	10
abuse (n)	12
acceptance	7
accusation	1
accuse	1, 6
accused, the (n)	1
actionable	3, 8
actus reus	5
adapted	6
adequate	7
adversarial	1
aggravated burglary	6
agreement	7, 11
appeal (n and v)	2
appropriate (v)	5, 6
appropriation	5
armed robbery	5
arrest (n and v)	3
assault (n)	3
auction (n)	7
authority	3, 6
B	
bar, the (n)	1
barrister	1
battery	3
binding (adj)	2
body	11
borrow	6
breach (n and v)	3, 7, 8, 9, 11
brief (n)	1
burden	8
burglary	3, 5
C	
capability	9
case law	4

	Unit
case	1
causation	10
caveat emptor	8
cede	11
charter (n)	12
citation	4
cite	4
citizenship	12
civil law	1
clause	7
coercive	11
collective	12
commit	6
commitment	12
common law	1, 9
compensation	9
competitive	7
compliance	11
component	5
compulsory	11
conduct (n)	9
conflict (n)	11
consent (n and v)	3, 5, 6
consideration	2, 7
constitute	8
constrain	3
constraint	3
constructive manslaughter	10
contempt	3
contentious	7
continuous service	9
contract (n)	1, 7
contractual obligation	7
contrary	6
convention	11, 12
conveyance	6
conviction	1, 2
copyright	12

	Unit
counter-offer	7
court	1
covenant	12
criminal (n and adj)	1
custodial	3
D	
damages	3, 8, 9
death penalty	10
deceit	5
deception	3, 5
declaration	11, 12
defamation	3
default (v)	8
defence (AmE defense)	1
defendant	1, 2
deliberate (adj)	5
deliberately	3, 5
deprive	3, 5, 6
detriment	7
diminished responsibility	10
disciplinary	9
discretion	8
discrimination	12
dishonest	1, 5
dishonestly	5
dishonesty	9
dismiss	9
display of goods	7
dispute (n and v)	3, 9, 11
doctrine	7, 8
domestic	11
E	
employment tribunal	9
enforce	1
enforceable	7
enforceablity	7

Transcripts

Unit 1, Lesson 2, Exercise B 🎧 1.1

Part 1

Welcome to the Law Faculty. I want to start my first lecture by asking a simple question. What is law? That's a very simple question, isn't it? We all know the answer – don't we? Let's see.

We know that the law provides a set of rules that allows people to live in an organized and civilized way. If someone breaks a rule, there's a system of punishment that not only protects people but also provides a deterrent. That is, it deters or stops people from breaking the rule. OK. But what are these rules and who decides what they are? For example, most people would agree that you should wash your hands before you eat a meal. If you don't, have you broken the law? In my household, my mother imposed this rule and if any of the children broke it, they were punished. But has someone who hasn't washed their hands before dinner broken the law? Well. Yes and no, or it depends. So what is law? What is the intrinsic meaning of the word? A word that we use every day and think we understand.

Unit 1, Lesson 2, Exercise C 🎧 1.2

Part 2

Many words have an intrinsic or basic meaning. We use the words in different situations and they have different surface meanings, but the basic meaning remains the same. Let's start with a word that is very familiar to many students: *bar*. We use the word *bar* to mean a place where you go to order drinks; a coffee bar, for example, or in a hotel you have a lounge bar. On the campus there are many student bars. But we also use the word *bar* in an English legal context. If you have been called to the bar, it means that you have the right to speak in court. In legal terminology, you are a barrister. Is there any connection between these two words? Yes, there is. A bar is a wooden stand from which a person can serve drinks, for example, in a hotel. In a court, it is also a wooden stand, not for serving drinks but where someone can speak to the court.

Somehow, when we're learning our first language, we get the feeling for the basic meaning of words which helps us to understand the same word in a new context. When we're learning another language, it's very important to find the basic meaning of a word because the direct translation in one context may not be the direct translation in another. For example, if you

directly translate the words *fair* and *just*, they may not have the same meaning as in a legal context. One of the basic meanings of *fair* is to describe a hair colour that is pale or not dark. *Just* often means *very recently*. These words are used with these meanings in the sentence: *My fair-haired sister has just arrived.* This is not the same as *a fair trial* or *a just outcome*. In this more legal context *fair* means that the trial is conducted in the right way and *just* means that the outcome was correct and appropriate.

Unit 1, Lesson 2, Exercise D 🎧 1.3

Part 3

So let me go back to my original question. What is law? We have criminal law, civil law, public law, international law, family law and company law. They are all elements of the set of rules which forbid, permit or require actions among people and organizations. They are all branches of the law. In my view many of the most important legal developments will take place in international law, and I'll talk in more detail about that in later lectures.

You will also study case law. In this context, a case refers to a binding or authoritative decision made by a court.

Unit 1, Lesson 2, Exercise E 🎧 1.4

Part 4

Let's look at this in a bit more detail. A case comes before a court in one of two ways. There is either a dispute between people in a civil case or between citizen and state in a criminal case. These cases are decided following a set of rules which forbid, allow or require people to do certain actions. These rules are then enforced.

Let's take an example that most people are familiar with. The law states that you must not drive more than 50 kilometres per hour in the centre of a town. If people drive at more than the 50 kilometres per hour speed limit they have broken the law, whether or not they get caught doing it. There is a reason for the law. It is dangerous to drive at more than 50 kilometres per hour in an area where people are walking and crossing the road.

If the driver is seen by the police or photographed by a speed camera, that driver will be prosecuted and punished. So this law helps people to live together in an organized and harmonious way. In fact, that is the meaning of the law in general. It is a set of rules that enables people to live together in an organized and we hope harmonious way.

Unit 1, Lesson 3, Exercise E 🎧 1.5

Introduction 1

OK, good morning, everyone. Today we're going to look at the way the court system in England and Wales is organized. Courts are generally classified into the criminal and the civil systems. The highest court in the land is known as the Supreme Court. It deals with both civil and criminal cases. The Supreme Court replaces the House of Lords, which sat as a court. Below the Supreme Court is the Court of Appeal. There are two separate divisions: civil and criminal. Below the Court of Appeal is the High Court.

Introduction 2

In this week's lecture we're going to be looking at the advantages and disadvantages of the jury system. A jury is a group of, usually, 12 ordinary people who have been selected to listen to the facts in a trial in a law court and decide on whether the case has been proved. It's claimed that the advantage of the jury system is that it ensures a fair trial, especially in criminal cases. People who are accused of an offence are tried by their peers – the general public rather than trained lawyers – who use their common sense to reach a verdict based solely on the evidence they have heard in the case. However, in recent years many lawyers have argued that the disadvantage of the jury system is that in some cases, such as serious fraud, the facts are generally too complex for the ordinary person in the street to follow.

Introduction 3

In this lecture I'm going to look at statutory interpretation. This is the way the courts construe or understand the meaning of the laws or statutes that have been passed by Parliament. However, the words that are used in statutes are not always precise, so judges need to interpret them to make sure they have understood the exact meaning that Parliament intended. In order to do this, judges use three rules, which are known as the literal rule, the mischief rule and the golden rule.

Introduction 4

In our legal history class today we're going to look at the development of statutory and common law within the English legal system. We're going to look at some of the significant dates in this historical development and what events occurred at those times. I think it's fair to say that most people, not just students, have difficulty remembering dates. However, there are some dates that are extremely significant and tend to stick in people's minds. Two of these dates in English history are 1066 and 1215.

In 1066 William the Conqueror invaded England from French Normandy and defeated the English King Harold at the Battle of Hastings. In 1215 the English King John was forced to sign a document known as the Magna Carta by the powerful lords and barons. I will explain why these dates are so important in the development of English law.

Introduction 5

Today we're going to look at the role of the solicitor and the kinds of functions a solicitor is likely to perform. A solicitor is generally the first point of contact for a person where the law is or is likely to be involved. This can be a legal transaction such as a house conveyance, a civil dispute such as a breach of contract or a possible prosecution where a person has been accused of breaking the law. The solicitor will advise the client on the course of action that needs to be taken.

Unit 1, Lesson 4, Exercise E 🎧 1.6

Lecture 1

The High Court is the highest court of first instance. There are three separate divisions: the Queen's Bench, the Chancery and the Family Division. Below the High Court on the civil side is the County Court and on the criminal side, the Crown Court. The County Court deals with relatively straightforward cases such as divorces and trespass to property. The Crown Court deals with serious criminal cases and appeals from the magistrates' court.

The magistrates' court is the lowest level court and has jurisdiction over a locality. It is presided over either by lay magistrates known as Justices of the Peace, or by a legally trained district judge. There are no juries.

Offenders who are aged between 10 and 17 are dealt with by Youth Courts with specially trained magistrates. These courts are not open to the public. Well, that's a brief overview of the court system. It's summarized on the PowerPoint slide.

Unit 1, Lesson 4, Exercise E 🎧 1.7

Lecture 2

There is also the problem of jury selection. Sitting on a jury is both a right and a duty. Jurors are selected at random from people who are entitled to vote who are under the age of 70. The advantage of this is that, in theory, juries are composed of people who come from a very wide spectrum of society. Unfortunately, many people try to avoid their duty because they claim they are too busy at work or will lose their salary. As a result, juries, it is argued, have too many people with time, such as unemployed and retired people, to provide a good balance.

Let us go back to the role of the jury. In a trial, the jury's function is to decide on the facts of the case. The jurors are there to determine the truth. However, many cases have a highly emotive element and this can, it is argued, sway the jury away from the facts.

Should emotion have a place in a court of law? Can a group of twelve ordinary men and women provide a fair trial and reach the correct verdict any better or worse than trained lawyers? The government is keen to abolish trial by jury for some crimes but surprisingly perhaps the legal profession is not. This, I think, is because we have an adversarial system where lawyers need to argue the case against each other.

Unit 1, Lesson 4, Exercise E 🎧 1.8

Lecture 3

The literal rule interprets words in their plain, ordinary dictionary meaning. This should mean that it is easier to come to a quick decision about what Parliament intended, as the word can be found in an easily available source. It also means that the judges should apply the words of Parliament. However, as we know, when you look up a word in a dictionary, it may still be open to wide interpretation.

The golden rule is a variation on the literal rule. When a word has multiple meanings, the judge selects one meaning that best fits the situation. In the Theft Act, section 1(1) states that 'a person is guilty of theft if he dishonestly appropriates property belonging to another'. The word *property* has many possible meanings and the judges have to interpret it in a way that best fits the situation in the case.

The court can also interpret a word so that the outcome of the trial is not unacceptable. In one case, a son would have benefited financially by murdering his mother. Under statute law, if a mother dies without making a will, the son must inherit. There is also a rule that no one can profit from their wrong. The court decided that using the literal rule would go against the wishes of Parliament and applied the golden rule instead.

The mischief rule looks at the law before the Act of Parliament was passed and what the Act was intended to change. Judges look at what mischief or wrongdoing Parliament intended to prevent rather than the exact words in the Act which might be open to interpretation.

Unit 1, Lesson 4, Exercise E 🎧 1.9

Lecture 4

Before the arrival of William the Conqueror in 1066, most laws in England were imposed by local communities and were enforced in many different ways. There was what was known as trial by ordeal. A person accused of a crime was given a piece of red hot metal to hold and if his hand burnt he was declared guilty! William attempted to impose the French codified legal system after 1066. This was not entirely successful and many laws were still only locally enforced. However, in 1154 Henry II created a unified system of law that was common to the whole country. This did away with these local differences and created a more powerful court system. It took some time for this system to work but since 1189, a date that is often referred to as 'time immemorial', English law has been described as a common law rather than a civil law system. When King John came to the throne he tried to assert the absolute power of the monarch over the existing legal system. He introduced higher taxes because in 1204 he had lost his lands in France and as a result a sizeable part of his income. This angered the powerful barons and eventually King John was forced to sign a document known as the Magna Carta in 1215. This was extremely significant in English legal history as it established the principle that there should be no imprisonment without trial. This is an issue that is still debated heatedly almost 800 years later.

Unit 1, Lesson 4, Exercise E 🎧 1.10

Lecture 5

Solicitors are not generally thought of as advocates. However, increasing numbers of solicitors are now becoming Higher Court advocates and the courts are widening their rights of audience to include solicitors. One of the functions of solicitors is to brief barristers. In other words, they collect all the legal documents that are necessary to enable the barrister to present the best case to the court. Solicitors usually work in partnerships, whereas barristers are what is known as sole practitioners. They work on their own.

Most people consult a solicitor when they want to buy or sell a house, when they want to write a will to distribute their money and property after their death, or to resolve a family dispute. People also consult their solicitor if they want to arrange a business contract or if they are setting up their own company. Some solicitors specialize in criminal work and make themselves available to people who have been arrested. I'm sure you've watched numerous films and TV programmes where someone says: 'I need a solicitor before I say another word.'

Unit 3, Lesson 2, Exercise B 🎧 1.11

Part 1

OK. Is everybody here? Right, let's start. What I'm going to talk about today is civil and criminal courts within the English legal system. Civil courts resolve disputes between private citizens or between private citizens and the state. In the criminal courts, cases are brought against a person who has broken the law. These cases are usually brought by the state. It is important to know the distinction between the cases that are heard in the civil court and the cases that are heard in the criminal court. So, in this lecture we're going to look at the differences and also where there is an overlap. We'll then take a brief look at tribunals and establish how these differ from civil and criminal courts.

Unit 3, Lesson 2, Exercise C 🎧 1.12

Part 2

Let's look at some examples to highlight the differences between the types of court. Firstly, trespass. Trespass is a tort, so the sign to deter unwanted visitors that you may have seen on a gate, 'Trespassers will be prosecuted', isn't correct. What's wrong with it? Remember, you can only prosecute someone in a criminal court, and trespass is not a crime. It's a tort. A trespasser would be sued in a civil court, and the court would normally order the defendant to pay damages. Or

in certain circumstances the court might issue a prohibitory injunction to prevent the trespasser from going onto the plaintiff's land. If there was a breach of the injunction, the trespasser would be in contempt of court and the case would be heard in either the county courts or the High Court.

What about assault? Well, assault is both a crime and a tort. In a criminal case, assault is usually defined as any act which intentionally or possibly recklessly causes another person to apprehend immediate and unlawful personal violence. 'Apprehend' means to understand that something is very likely to happen. Battery, on the other hand, is usually defined as the intentional or reckless application of force on another person. If you deliberately bump into someone in a street, that would be actionable, but if the street was extremely crowded and you had no way of avoiding it, that would be part of acceptable social interaction and would probably not be actionable.

Theft is a crime and is defined in the Theft Act 1968 as 'dishonestly appropriating the property of another with the intention of permanently depriving the other of it.' Here is a situation which, sadly, some of you might have experienced. A student was on his first visit to the UK and was unfamiliar with the currency. He took a taxi and paid the driver what he thought was the correct sum of money. The driver indicated that he needed more and took notes from the student's wallet that amounted to far more than the actual fare. The driver was convicted of theft and appealed on the grounds that the victim consented to the money being taken. The Appeal Court judges rejected this argument because the student only consented to the legal amount being taken.

Unit 3, Lesson 2, Exercise D 🎧 1.13

Part 3

Cases brought before the civil courts are to do with legal matters such as breach of contract, trespass to property, and disputes over land or the wrongful exercise of power by a public authority. Cases are usually cited with the names of the parties to the dispute: for example, *Miller and Jackson*. This is written *Miller* **v** *Jackson*, but said as 'and': *Miller **and** Jackson.*

In civil cases, the court can award damages to the person who has suffered as the result of wrongdoing. In certain circumstances, the court will issue an injunction to prevent the wrongdoing from occurring again.

Cases brought before the criminal courts are to do with offences against the state which, these days, usually involve breach of the statutory law. In the UK, cases in the criminal courts are cited as *R* v *Smith*; *R* stands for *Regina* or the Crown against Smith. When lawyers refer to criminal cases they often use just the name of the accused: for example, *Smith*. If the accused is found guilty, the court can order punishment. This can either be a custodial sentence, which means going to prison, or a non-custodial sentence such as a fine, probation or a community service order.

Remember that a court is different from a tribunal, although the distinction is not always clear. The House of Lords decided in *Attorney General* v *BBC* [1980] that a court exercises the judicial power of the state. If it only has an administrative function, it is not a court. This distinction is not merely semantic as it has a direct bearing on contempt of court proceedings. Contempt of court, by definition, applies only to courts of justice and not to other legal decision-making bodies. It has been held that an Employment Appeal Tribunal which would hear cases of wrongful dismissal by an employer is a court; yet there can be no contempt of court in a tribunal.

Unit 3, Lesson 2, Exercise E 🎧 1.14

Part 4

So, to summarize. In the English legal system there are three different types of court: civil courts, criminal courts and tribunals which act as courts. We have looked at the cases that are likely to be heard in each type of court. Trespass is a tort and the plaintiff will sue in the civil courts. Assault can be both a crime and a tort, and the case could be brought in either the civil court or the criminal court, depending on the circumstances. In a civil case of assault the plaintiff will sue for damages while in a criminal case the police might charge a person with grievous bodily harm. Theft is a crime, and cases of theft are heard in the criminal courts.

Tribunals which act as courts and have a judicial rather than administrative function include the Employment Appeal Tribunal. This tribunal would hear cases of wrongful dismissal by an employer, for example.

OK, that's it for today. Next time, we'll look in detail at trespass to the person. Don't forget to do a bit of research on that before you come. Thanks. See you soon.

Unit 3, Lesson 2, Exercise F 🎧 1.15

1 Theft is a tort.
2 The usual remedy for trespass to property is for the court to award damages.
3 Cases involving a breach of contract would be heard in the criminal court.
4 A community service order is a type of non-custodial sentence.
5 Courts have only an administrative function.
6 If a case is cited as the Crown against Smith it will be heard in a civil court.

Unit 3, Lesson 3, Exercise A 🎧 1.16

1 'wrongdoing
2 in'junction
3 dis'pute
4 'trespass
5 'reckless
6 'prosecute
7 pro'hibitory
8 defa'mation
9 'damages
10 cus'todial
11 dis'honest
12 'criminal
13 con'tempt
14 'battery
15 a'ssault
16 'justice
17 de'liberately
18 'permanently

Unit 3, Lesson 4, Exercise B 🎧 1.17

Part 1

In the last lecture, we talked about trespass as a tort. As you'll remember, trespass is the intentional wrongdoing to a person or to property. In this lecture, we're going to look in more detail at trespass to the person. There are three types of trespass to the person: assault, battery and false imprisonment.

Assault is an act which intentionally causes another person to expect that unlawful force will be used. Battery is the actual infliction of unlawful force on another person. False imprisonment is unlawfully constraining someone against their will in a particular place.

Let's concentrate today on what this tort is and what the defences to it are.

Unit 3, Lesson 4, Exercise C 🎧 1.18

Part 2

In strict legal language, assault is causing the apprehension of the application of unlawful force. This means that someone intends to apply force to another person, and that person reasonably expects that this will happen. Let's look at intention. If someone shakes their clenched fist at another person, but is stopped from hitting that person by the intervention of a third party, there will be a case as the person shaking the clenched fist intended to commit a violent act. However, the claimant must have reasonably expected an immediate battery. It has also been argued that words alone can constitute an assault.

OK. Now, battery involves the infliction of unlawful force. In theory, merely touching a person in anger could constitute battery. If you unintentionally touch someone on a crowded underground train, this is unlikely to amount to battery. However, if you deliberately push them out of the way in order to get to the train door before it closes, you might be liable.

False imprisonment is unlawfully constraining someone against their will in a particular place. For example, a customer hasn't paid for some goods in a shop, and the shopkeeper detains them for quite a long period of time. This might be seen as false imprisonment.

Unit 3, Lesson 4, Exercise D 🎧 1.19

Part 3

What about the defences to trespass to the person? The first line of defence is consent. Consent can be given expressly by words or can be implied by the action a person takes. If you play a contact sport, such as football or rugby, you expect to have a degree of physical contact when, for example, you are tackled or jostling to get the ball. By taking part in the sport, you consent by implication to this physical contact. However, if you are punched in the face by an opponent, this is not part of the normal run of play. It isn't, after

all, a boxing match! It would not be a defence that you consented to being punched just because you played in the game, as you couldn't reasonably expect this to happen during or even after the game. It has been argued that in a sport such as ice hockey, punching other players, although against the rules, is all part of the game and therefore if you play ice hockey you might reasonably expect to be punched during the course of the game!

Lawful arrest is also a defence. If person A reasonably expects that person B is likely to commit a breach of the peace – that is to harm or threaten to harm someone – A has the right to prevent the breach of the peace from taking place by restraining B against B's will. However, the police or the private citizen making the arrest must not act unlawfully.

Self-defence is a long-established defence under the common law. A person may use 'reasonable force' to protect himself, his property or his land from interference. The court has to decide on what reasonable force is. For example, it may decide that it is not reasonable force to fire a shotgun with live bullets at people trespassing on an owner's land. However, what is reasonable will always depend on the exact circumstances.

Necessity is another line of defence. This defence is often used in cases involving medical treatment. If a doctor acts to preserve the life of a patient, even without the patient's consent, it would not be trespass, provided that the doctor acted reasonably. If you see someone about to be run over by a car, you would immediately try to push them out of the way. You wouldn't wait to ask their permission!

Unit 3, Lesson 4, Exercise E 🎧 1.20

Part 4

So, to recap, we are looking at the tort of trespass to the person. There are three types: assault, battery and false imprisonment. There is a range of defences available. These include consent, lawful arrest, self-defence and necessity.

The case law on trespass to the person is extensive. I would suggest you start your research with some of the 19th-century cases I've referenced on the PowerPoint slides.

Unit 5, Lesson 2, Exercise B 🎧 1.21

Part 1

Good morning, everyone. This morning we're going to begin the topic of theft. In this first talk, I'm just going to give you an overview of a few key concepts, and then I'll go into more detail on the different types of theft over the course of the next few lectures. Also, in your seminars and assignments you'll be able to cover all the important points in more detail. So ... er ... let's see ... yes.

To start with, we need to consider what theft is. In other words, what is the legal definition of theft? Secondly, what are the components of theft – the *actus reus* and *mens rea*. That is, on the one hand, the appropriation, and, on the other, the intention of doing something dishonestly.

Thirdly, I'll mention some of the offences of theft, because it isn't just stealing property. After that, I'll discuss some of the defences to a charge of theft, and I'll finish by mentioning the important case law.

Unit 5, Lesson 2, Exercise D 🎧 1.22

Part 2

Well, what is theft? Let's look again at the definition given in the Theft Act 1968. Section 1(1) creates the offence of theft. It states: 'A person is guilty of theft if he dishonestly appropriates property belonging to another with the intention of permanently depriving the other of it.' I'll give that definition again. 'A person is guilty of theft if he dishonestly appropriates property belonging to another with the intention of permanently depriving the other of it.' There are obviously a number of words and phrases here which have to be interpreted by the court in any particular case, particularly *appropriates*, *property*, and *intention to permanently deprive*.

The definition of 'appropriation' is provided by section 3(1), which states: 'Any assumption by a person of the *rights* of an owner amounts to an appropriation, and this includes, where he has come by the property (innocently or not) without stealing it, any later assumption of a right to it by keeping or dealing with it as an owner.'

The word 'property' in general English often means a house or a flat, but, of course, in legal terms the definition is much wider, and includes anything which is owned, including intangible things, things which you can't touch, like the

intellectual rights to an invention or a piece of art or literature. Section 4(1) of the Act states that property includes money and all other property, real or personal, including intangible property. So, for example, patents for new products and trademarks for goods, like McDonald's, are intangible property and can be misappropriated under the terms of the Act.

With regard to 'permanently deprive', this in effect means to treat a thing as your own to dispose of, regardless of the other's rights. In this respect, the length of time for which the thing is taken is not necessarily important.

OK. Now, what about actual offences? In fact, we're going to look at this in a lot more detail next time, but today I will mention a few of the most important offences. Firstly, there's shoplifting, which, of course, means taking things from shops without paying for them. Interestingly, some shops actually have signs up now which say, 'Shoplifting is theft.' And maybe, 'We always prosecute.' This is because some people have the wrong idea that shoplifting is a victimless crime – nobody really suffers, particularly if you take things from a very big shop. But, actually, we all suffer from shoplifting because the shops have to charge more for everything to cover the cost of the things that are stolen. Where was I? Oh yes ... shoplifting. A second offence is sometimes called TWOC – taking without the owner's consent. This often applies to stealing a car. Thirdly, there's burglary and fourthly armed robbery. I shall say a lot more about these next time.

Oh, sorry. I should have mentioned the components of theft. Firstly, the *actus reus*, or guilty deed, of theft consists of the appropriation of property belonging to another as just defined. Then there is the *mens rea*, or the guilty mind, which in theft is also fundamental. The *mens rea* consists of the defendant acting, firstly, dishonestly and, secondly, with the intention of permanently depriving.

Let's see how this can operate in practice. Although theft usually occurs when a person takes property belonging to somebody else, there are many other situations where theft can arise. For example, John lends a book to Mary. If Mary then sells or even gives the book to Peter, she will have appropriated the book and may therefore be guilty of theft. Only John, who is the owner of the book, has the right to sell or give the book away. We shall, of course, consider some of the defences later on, such as acting in good faith.

Unit 5, Lesson 2, Exercise E 🎧 1.23

Part 3

Let's look now at some of the defences to theft. Firstly, what is acting dishonestly? The Theft Act section 2 doesn't give a precise definition of dishonesty, but identifies what it is *not*. According to the Act, there are three elements to this. A person does not act dishonestly if he appropriates property in the belief that:

> firstly, he has in law the right to deprive the other of it; or …

> secondly, he would have the other's consent; or …

> thirdly, the person to whom the property belongs cannot be discovered by taking reasonable steps.

So, for example, if you find someone's mobile phone on a train seat, there are reasonable steps you can take to discover the owner by, for example, dialling one of the numbers. If you keep the phone, you may be guilty of theft. But if you find a book on a train seat, and there is no name inside, what can you do? How can you find out the owner? Er … where was I? Yes, yes. It may *not* be a defence to say you are willing to pay for the thing. It may still be construed as dishonest appropriation. For example, imagine that John lends Mary a book. If Mary sells the book to Bill and then offers to pay John the money she got from Bill, she may still be guilty of theft.

Unit 5, Lesson 3, Exercise B 🎧 1.24

Part 4

So how do the courts deal with cases involving theft? By applying the rules of statutory interpretation. Actually, the Theft Act is arguably one of the most important laws on the statute book. So, it follows that the courts must ensure that cases involving theft are properly interpreted. What I mean is, they are interpreted in the way in which Parliament intended. Fundamentally, the courts have had to interpret a number of key words, which have at times caused judges some difficulty. Anyway, er … to return to the main point, it's essential to identify the basic components that make up the crime of theft. Naturally, it is the aim of all judges to interpret the statute in a just and fair way.

There are several important cases where the key words I have identified have needed to be interpreted. The courts have had to consider factors such as honest and dishonest appropriation. However … oh, dear … sadly, I see that we've run out of time. This means that I'll have to ask *you* to do some research. I'd like you to find out the way in which the courts have interpreted the key concepts of the Theft Act that I've mentioned: acting dishonestly, appropriation, permanently depriving and consent. I'm going to talk in some detail next time about the House of Lords case, *R* v *Hinks* [2000], but I'd like you to do some research into two other important cases which set precedents, that's *Gomez* which was … um … 1992 … no, '93. That was also in the House of Lords. And finally *Lawrence*. Let's see, that was '72, wasn't it? Yes, 1972 in the Appeal Court. We'll discuss what you've found out next time I see you.

Unit 5, Lesson 3, Exercise C 🎧 1.25

1 in'terpret
2 a'ppropriate
3 a'ssumption
4 de'fence
5 a'ssignment
6 'precedent
7 defi'nition
8 com'ponent
9 'statutory
10 de'prive
11 in'tangible
12 'property

Unit 5, Lesson 3, Exercise D 🎧 1.26

Actually, the Theft Act 1968 is arguably one of the most important laws on the statute book. So, it follows that the courts must ensure that cases involving theft are properly interpreted. What I mean is, they're interpreted in the way in which Parliament intended. Fundamentally, the courts have had to interpret a number of key words, which have at times caused judges some difficulty. Anyway, to return to the main point, it's essential to identify the basic components that make up the crime of theft. Naturally, it is the aim of all judges to interpret the statute in a just and fair way.

Unit 5, Lesson 4, Exercise B 🎧 1.27

Extract 1

LECTURER: Right, Leila and Majed, what did you find out about the cases involving dishonesty as defined by the Theft Act 1968?

LEILA: Well, first of all, we looked at the well-known case of *R* v *Hinks* in the House of Lords.

MAJED: I went to the House of Lords last year. It's amazing!

Extract 2

LECTURER: And what else did you do?

LEILA: We did a bit more research into other cases that were cited in the original transcript.

MAJED: That's rubbish. We just found out something about it on the Internet.

Extract 3

LECTURER: Leila, can you give us an explanation about why *Hinks* is such an important case?

LEILA: Well, yes. It established the way in which honesty and appropriation are interpreted. The court decided that the defendant appropriated a sum of £60,000, even though she claimed the money had been given to her as a gift.

LECTURER: What do the rest of you make of this? Evie, what about you?

EVIE: Well, erm … I'm not sure really.

Extract 4

LECTURER: Majed, can you explain how the court interpreted the word *appropriate* under the terms of the Theft Act?

MAJED: I think they decided that you can still steal money from a person, even if the owner willingly hands it over.

JACK: It's like cheating someone.

Extract 5

LECTURER: What did the court decide about the defendant's dishonesty, Jack?

JACK: The defendant lost the case, but one of the dissenting judges stated that it was not common sense to say that someone who had received money as a gift had acted dishonestly, and …

EVIE: So the court decided she wasn't dishonest.

Unit 5, Lesson 4, Exercise C 🎧 1.28

Extract 6

LECTURER: Let's go back to the facts of the case in *Hinks* for the moment, to see how it can help us understand this key matter of appropriation. First of all, tell us what this case was actually about.

LEILA: Well, Miss Hinks, the defendant, looked after a guy called John Dolphin. He wasn't very bright, was he, Majed?

MAJED: That's right. He was described in court as *naïve*. He also had no real idea of how much money he had.

Extract 7

MAJED: John Dolphin wrote out a cheque for £60,000 and deposited it in Miss Hinks' bank account. It was said that, although he was of limited intelligence, he was still capable of making a gift and understanding the concept of ownership.

JACK: Sorry, I don't follow. Could you possibly explain why that's important?

MAJED: Well, basically, Miss Hinks believed that if she could prove it was a genuine gift, she couldn't be found guilty of theft.

Extract 8

EVIE: I don't understand how she could have been charged with theft if John Dolphin gave her the money.

LEILA: Well, it's like a con man in the street.

EVIE: You mean a cheater?

LEILA: Yes, you know, like Find the Lady. You give him the money willingly, but it's a trick. So, really, he has stolen the money from you.

Extract 9

MAJED: Yes, the case finally went to the House of Lords where a majority of the judges decided that in a prosecution for theft it was unnecessary to prove it was done without the owner's consent.

JACK: If I understand you correctly, you're saying that a person can still be found guilty of theft, even if the owner of what they have stolen has agreed to that person taking it.

MAJED: Yes, that's right.

Extract 10

LECTURER: This is all very interesting, isn't it?

EVIE: Yes, because this judgment shows that lack of

consent is not essential to a charge of theft. I can give you something willingly, but you may have still stolen it from me!

LEILA: Correct!

Unit 7, Lesson 2, Exercise B 🎧 1.29

Part 1

Good morning, everyone. What I'm going to talk about today is one of the key elements in the formation of a contract under English law: consideration. Consideration is the requirement that for parties to be able to enforce a promise, something must be given or promised in exchange or return for the promise. Firstly, we're going to look at what is known as the doctrine of consideration. That is, where, how and why consideration is applied in the formation of a contract. Then we're going to look at how consideration is used to make a contract enforceable. A contract is enforceable where parties can be compelled to fulfil their obligations through the legal process. Next we're going to look at what are known as executory and executed contracts and how they relate to the doctrine of consideration. An executory contract occurs when someone promises to do something. For example, X promises that he'll mend Y's car next week and charge the usual hourly rate. An executed contract occurs when the work which the parties agreed to has been carried out. Y does not pay X the usual hourly rate until the car has been mended. However, the amount of money or the consideration for the work was agreed before the work was started. This is very important in legal terms. For example, X agrees to mend Y's car because he enjoys mending cars and initially says he does not want any payment. He completes the work and then demands that Y gives him the usual hourly rate. In this situation the consideration is now past, as the work has already been completed. Finally, we will look at the case law to see how judges have interpreted the ways in which consideration is applied.

The doctrine of consideration applies only within the English legal system. In other words, consideration is not a strict requirement for the formation of a contract under other common law jurisdictions such as Scottish, Australian or United States law. Bearing in mind that this doctrine is initially difficult to grasp, plus the complex case law that relates to it, let us look at exactly what consideration is. As I said at the beginning of the lecture, consideration is the requirement that for parties to be able to enforce a promise, something must be given or promised in exchange or return for the promise. This is also known as the *quid pro quo*. What I mean is, the contract must be met with or supported by consideration. It's often in the form of monetary benefit. However, the consideration must not just be a gratuitous promise where someone promises something that is obviously not intended to be legally binding. I'm sure we've all said things when we're desperate, like 'If you can mend my car, I'll give you a million pounds.' The court is extremely unlikely to hold that this statement would result in the formation of a contract.

The general rule is that the promisor obtains or will obtain some right, interest, profit or benefit which is a direct result of some forbearance, detriment, loss or responsibility suffered or undertaken by the promisee. X promises to mend Y's car. If X gets the car to work, Y agrees to drive X wherever he wants for the next month. X gets the benefit of free car journeys and Y has to give up his time and money in order to provide the service he has agreed to. Y suffers a detriment. The *quid pro quo* is, of course, that Y gets his car mended.

Unit 7, Lesson 2, Exercise C 🎧 1.30

Part 2

As we've seen in the introduction to this lecture, consideration is a requirement for the formation of a contract under English law. It can be thought of in simple terms as getting something back for what you've done. As we know, people rarely do something for nothing! Remember, another term for this is the Latin phrase *quid pro quo*. As well as consideration there must, of course, be the offer, acceptance and the intention to form legal relations. In other words, for a legal contract to be formed, all of these elements must be in place.

The importance of consideration in the formation of a contract is illustrated in *Roscorla* v *Thomas* (1842) 3 QB 234. In this case, Roscorla bought a horse from Thomas. After the sale was completed, Thomas promised that the horse was 'sound'; that is, in good condition. The horse turned out to be a vicious, nasty beast. It was held that Roscorla could not enforce the promise made by Thomas, as the consideration for entering into the contract had been completed by the time the promise that the horse was sound had been made. In order for this promise to be enforceable Roscorla would need to offer fresh consideration. So, the consideration must usually be made before the contract is completed. In this way, the consideration is a *quid pro quo* for a promise that is made which can then be enforceable under the contract.

Unit 7, Lesson 2, Exercise E 🎧 1.31

Part 3

OK then. An important concept is that of past consideration. What do I mean by past consideration? As you can see from *Roscorla* v *Thomas*, there was a contract for the sale of a horse. At the time the contract was made, the condition the horse was in was not an issue. Looking at it another way, the consideration for the original sale was the sum of money Roscorla paid for the horse. Subsequently, when Thomas promised that the horse was sound, Roscorla already owned the horse and did not offer anything in return for this promise. In legal terms, there was no enforceable contract.

Let's look at another example of this. Say X rents a flat from Y. While living in the flat X redecorates it. After all the work has been completed Y agrees to pay X a sum of money for the work done. Y then breaks this promise to X. The contract is unenforceable because the promise was made after the decorating was completed. The point is that the consideration must be either for something to be done in the future, known as an executory contract, or for something that is actually completed, known as an executed contract.

For example, Y pays X money to decorate the flat next week. If X fails to do the work the contract is enforceable because the agreement was made and the consideration established before the work was carried out. This is an executory contract. Or, if Y agrees to pay X a sum of money when the decoration is completed and X carries out the work satisfactorily, the contract has been carried out or executed. So this is an executed contract. The important point is that the consideration must be current and must not be used up before the promise is made.

Unit 7, Lesson 2, Exercise F 🎧 1.32

Part 4

Now … er … let's see … oh dear, I see we're running short of time … but perhaps I should just say something about past consideration. The basic rule is that past consideration is insufficient to form a contract. One exception is the later promise. If a later promise can be linked to the initial request, the consideration for the later promise can be treated as all part of one agreement.

The old case of *Lampleigh* v *Braithwaite* illustrates this. What this case demonstrates is that the court can consider later promises.

Braithwaite killed someone and then asked Lampleigh to get him a pardon. A pardon is when the monarch forgives someone for a crime that has been committed. Lampleigh successfully petitioned the king and Braithwaite was granted a pardon. Braithwaite then promised to pay Lampleigh for what he had done. However, Braithwaite broke his promise and did not pay Lampleigh. What the court held was extremely significant. Although Lampleigh's consideration was past, as he had already got the pardon, it could be implied that at the time of Braithwaite's initial request to get a pardon there was an understanding that Lampleigh would be paid.

Also, no consideration is needed when there is a modification or change to the existing contract. This is highlighted in the case of *Williams* v *Roffey Brothers*. I'll give you the citation so you can look it up … It's [1991] 1 QB 1.

Now … oh dear … I was going to mention the other rules of consideration. These are … uh … quite complicated but … uh … time is moving on. So instead, I'm going to …

Unit 7, Lesson 3, Exercise A 🎧 1.33

1 obli'gation
2 in'tention
3 'detriment
4 ex'ecutory
5 per'formance
6 'contract
7 'doctrine
8 suf'ficient
9 'promise
10 en'force
11 consider'ation
12 'privity

Unit 7, Lesson 3, Exercise B 🎧 1.34

Part 5

I'm going to finish with some comments on how judges have interpreted consideration – in other words, the case law. Now the fact of the matter is that the case law is highly complex. The reason for this is that in any agreement there are a number of different factors; not to mention the fact that judges can interpret these factors in different ways. We've already seen this in the cases involving past consideration. Let's take what the courts have decided to be good consideration. For consideration to be good it must be *sufficient*. That means it is measurable in economic terms. However, it does not have to be *adequate*. That is, in economic terms, what the offeree gives does not have to match what the offeror thinks is the real value.

OK. Where was I? Oh yes – good consideration. The courts have interpreted good consideration in a number of ways: payment, provision of a service, et cetera. For example, you've probably heard of the famous chocolate manufacturer Nestlé. It was in the case of *Chappell* v *Nestlé* that what amounted to adequate consideration was discussed. The facts of the case were that as an advertising promotion, the chocolate company, Nestlé, offered to sell records of a popular song to customers in return for a very small sum of money and three chocolate wrappers. The copyright to the records was owned by Chappell and they claimed that they were entitled to royalties on the sales of these records under the Copyright Act 1956. The royalties were based on the 'retail price'. It was held that the wrappers, though worthless in themselves, amounted to good consideration because the purchasers of the chocolate bars, the offerees, had given something adequate to the company, the offeror.

To sum up, then, the point is that the law recognizes that consideration must have some economic value even though this economic value cannot be precisely quantified.

Oh, I almost forgot to mention your research topics. OK, well, one important aspect of consideration is how it is affected by the doctrine of privity of contract. The doctrine of privity of contract means that a contract is only enforceable by the parties who made the contract, normally known as the promisor and the promisee, and not by third parties. A good starting point to understand this doctrine is the case of *Dunlop* v *Selfridge* [1915]. Also, how the common law doctrine laid down in this case should be interpreted in the light of legislation such as the Contracts (Rights of Third Parties) Act 1999. I'd like you to find out the main criteria for deciding who is permitted to sue under the terms of a contract.

Unit 7, Lesson 4, Exercise B 🎧 1.35

Extract 1

OK, so what we'll be discussing now is how judges have interpreted what good consideration is. Now, as we know, consideration under English law is a requirement for the formation of a contract. Last time I asked you to look at the contentious case of *Williams* v *Roffey Brothers* [1991] 1 QB 1. What was decided in this case, and why was it contentious? Under common law, an agreement cannot be enforced without consideration, and performance of an existing contractual duty is not consideration. However, in this case the Court of Appeal held that the new agreement conferred additional practical benefit on Roffey by enabling the company to avoid the penalty clause. So the judges appeared to be saying that a contract is enforceable even if there is no consideration. Now, I'd like to hear your views.

Unit 7, Lesson 4, Exercises C and D 🎧 1.36

Extract 2

JACK: Well. I'd like to make two points. First, If you do something that is already required under a contract you're not entitled to additional payment.

LEILA: Can you expand on that, Jack?

JACK: Sure, Leila. In the case of Stilk and Myrick the sailors demanded extra wages because they had to do the work of two other sailors who had run away from the ship. The court held that they weren't entitled to the money as there was no consideration. So the point is that you cannot enforce a promise to pay you additional money for work you have already agreed to do.

LECTURER: OK. So, what's your second point, Jack?

JACK: I was coming to that! My second point is that in the Williams and Roffey Brothers case, Williams did give Roffey consideration because Roffey managed to avoid paying out under the penalty clause. Williams had provided a practical benefit.

LEILA: Yes, but that's true in Stilk and Myrick too. Even more so, I'd say. They had to work really hard to get the ship back to England, which is definitely a practical benefit.

MAJED: Well, I don't agree with that, Leila, because from what I've read, the judge in the Stilk case decided that the sailors had already agreed to do the work.

EVIE: Sorry, but what are we talking about, exactly? Doing something you have already agreed to do or doing something which gives the other party practical benefit?

LEILA: Yes, we need to be clear here. Additional payment can only be enforced if the person doing the work provides a practical benefit, I think. Anyway, I'd just like to say that according to what I've read, in the Williams case the subcontractor did provide a practical benefit.

EVIE: In what way?

LEILA: Well, he finished the work on time and did a good job. Also, he enabled Roffey to avoid paying the penalty clause.

EVIE: I don't get that. Wasn't that a requirement under the original contract?

LEILA: What I'm trying to say is, Williams did more than he was originally asked to do.

MAJED: I still don't understand. Can you give me an example, Leila?

LEILA: OK. Look at it this way. I agree to mend your car and you offer to buy me dinner in return for the work I have done. I enjoy mending cars but the work takes longer to do than I thought. You offer to pay me some money as you want the car for the weekend. I get the car working and that evening you take me out to dinner. You then drive off and don't pay me the money. I have provided you with a practical benefit because you get the car for the weekend.

MAJED: So, the promise to pay extra money has to be supported by consideration?

LECTURER: Absolutely. In making a decision about a contract, the courts have to think about whether there is good consideration provided by a practical benefit which is more than just the performance of an existing contractual duty.

MAJED: Yes, and I'd just like to say something else. As I mentioned before, the judgment in the Stilk case is still considered to be sound and Williams and Roffey does not overturn it. Although the Williams case challenges the traditional view of consideration, it has not been followed by judges in many other cases.

Unit 9, Lesson 2, Exercise B 🎧 2.1

Part 1

Good morning, everyone. I'm going to talk to you this morning about dismissal from employment, and in particular, two important types of dismissal. These two types are known as unfair dismissal and wrongful dismissal. As you can probably guess from the names, they are both claims against employers – ways in which employees can seek redress if they have been sacked by their employers or have lost their jobs in other ways.

In this lecture, I'm going to compare and contrast the two kinds of claim. First, I'll talk about unfair dismissal, and then I'll go on to wrongful dismissal. But, because there are great similarities, I will make points about both kinds throughout the lecture.

But before we begin I have a little story to tell you … I once worked for a small legal company with a very dynamic boss who had lots of good ideas and was very good with people. However, he wasn't very good at the financial side of the company. He didn't like working with numbers and details and he was very forgetful. His financial management was terrible and I lost my job after a year because the company went bust. Of course, in that case, I didn't have a claim for unfair dismissal or wrongful dismissal, but the point of that story is that, through no fault of their own, employees can lose their jobs. And if this happens, it's important for employees to know what action they can take to obtain compensation.

So, to get back to the main part of my lecture. Now to start with, as we've already noted, it's clear that people can lose their jobs in a variety of different circumstances. Increasingly we find that when people do lose their jobs, especially when they believe it's through no fault of their own, they want to know how the law will protect them. In fact, as we will see, the courts provide protection in a number of ways.

At the beginning of the lecture I mentioned two types of dismissal: unfair dismissal and wrongful dismissal. It's the first of these, unfair dismissal, that I'm going to focus on now, although it's worth pointing out that in certain circumstances an unfair dismissal can also be a wrongful dismissal and vice versa. I'll give you some of the important case law citations later on.

OK, so to start with, let's take a few moments to consider the key point about unfair dismissal. What is unfair dismissal? Firstly, unfair dismissal is a statutory invention. In other words, it didn't exist until it became part of statutory law. It's a relatively new concept, as it only came into force in the Industrial Relations Act of 1971. By contrast, wrongful dismissal, which we will come to later, is subject to common law. Cases involving unfair dismissal are heard in employment tribunals and not in the ordinary courts. There is one key point before we look at the detail: normally an employee needs to have at least a year's continuous service before being able to claim unfair dismissal.

Now, in terms of the contract of employment, the employer must have a good reason for dismissing the employee and has to show that the reason is genuine and justifies the dismissal. There are a number of potentially fair reasons for an employer to dismiss an employee, such as conduct and capability. We'll look in more detail at these reasons later. Incidentally, it could be argued that these reasons for dismissal might also occur in wrongful dismissal. However, remember that, in theory, the remedy for unfair dismissal is only available if an employee has more than one year's continuous service. As we shall see, the courts take a different approach when employees have lost their jobs after being with a company for less than a year.

So, there are a variety of circumstances in which an employee can claim unfair dismissal. For example: your boss asks you to perform a task that you think is outside the range of skills which you were employed for. You do the task badly and, as a result, you're fired. In these circumstances, if the tribunal accepts that you were not offered or provided with adequate training to perform the task, *and* the task was outside your job description, it might conclude that you were unfairly dismissed, provided you had completed one year's continuous service. It could be argued that the management simply believed that the employee was incompetent and unable to carry out the task, regardless of whether or not training was offered. It is then up to the tribunal to decide, on the facts, if the dismissal was unfair.

As I said, unfair dismissal is a statutory matter so the levels of compensation awarded in the event of an unfair dismissal are fixed by statute: that is to say, the maximum awards are usually calculated by a formula, such as multiples of one week's pay.

There is one other important point. Employers must act fairly in the procedure they follow during the dismissal. They must follow certain dismissal procedures before they can lawfully dismiss a person who has 12 months' service or more. If they don't, the dismissal is automatically unfair. Even if you don't have 12 months' service, if they sack you because, for example, you're pregnant, join a trade union or complain about a health and safety problem, that is unfair dismissal. This is all laid down in various statutory provisions.

Oh, one final point, very important, in relation to unfair dismissal is that, unlike wrongful dismissal, it can occur without any breach of contract. What I mean is, an unfair dismissal can occur even though the employer has not broken the terms of the contract.

Unit 9, Lesson 2, Exercise C 🎧 2.2

Part 2

OK. Let's turn now to wrongful dismissal. In wrongful dismissal cases, the employer has breached the terms of the contract by, for example, failing to give the correct period of notice, or failing to provide adequate compensation instead of the period of notice. Wrongful dismissal may also occur if an employee resigns from the job because the employer has committed a serious breach of contract, and the employee has not waived the breach by, for example, staying in the same job for too long after the breach was committed. Waiving in this case – W-A-I-V-I-N-G – means ignoring the breach. If you think a breach of contract by your employer is a serious matter, you must react quickly, otherwise the courts may decide that you waived, or ignored, the breach. From the point of view of the contract, a serious breach would be something like a complete change of the job description or a substantial reduction in pay.

Leading on from the previous point, wrongful dismissal cases follow the common law rules of contract. An employer has defences against wrongful dismissal if an employee has committed gross misconduct by, for example, stealing company property. In such a case, the employer has the right to sack the employee without notice. Of course, it's true to say that the same reason can also be given in cases of unfair dismissal because your employer has a genuine reason which justifies your dismissal.

As you can see, there are many similarities between unfair dismissal and wrongful dismissal, but crucially there are a number of differences. Let us recap. Unfair dismissal is an invention of statute. In order to claim unfair dismissal, an employee must normally have at least one year's continuous service. Cases for unfair dismissal are heard in an employment tribunal, and there is a cap on the maximum allowable amount for compensation. On the other hand, wrongful dismissal is governed by the rules of common law, and cases of wrongful dismissal are normally heard in the ordinary courts such as the county court or the High Court.

As we have seen, wrongful dismissal follows the rules of the common law. And in that sense, of course, the precedents set in the case law are very important and you will need to study the facts in the cases I refer to very carefully in order to understand how the judges have interpreted, for example, breaches of contract. Thus, in wrongful dismissal cases, the judges are not concerned with the statutory provisions *per se* but in the application of the principles established by the common law. These can be quite complex, as you can see in the case of *Gunton v Richmond-upon-Thames* [1980]. Briefly, the facts of the case were that Gunton was employed as a college registrar and was dismissed from his employment because he was subject to disciplinary procedures. Gunton sued for wrongful dismissal on the grounds that he was not given notice. Previous cases established that even if an employee is wrongfully dismissed, he is only entitled to claim for damages for the loss of salary he would have received instead of notice. He is not entitled to sue for damages for the demeaning way in which the dismissal occurred, or for any loss of reputation caused by the dismissal. The common law rule of mitigation also applies. The sacked employee is under a duty to mitigate the loss of salary by looking for alternative employment.

You may consider that the common law appears to favour the employer rather than the employee. Research has shown that in fact the courts did frequently find in favour of the employer. If you study the relevant transcripts you will see a number of references to the master/servant relationship. Many of the earlier cases were, of course, heard during the Victorian period in 19th-century Britain, when about a third of the working population worked in domestic service. In those days, it could be argued that the employers' rights were upheld because the judges belonged to the same class and had domestic servants themselves.

Now, where was I? Oh yes, right, I was talking about the importance of the rules of common law in cases involving wrongful dismissal. It was held that Gunton was only entitled to damages for loss of salary. He was dismissed by his employer,

therefore his contract came to an end. He was entitled to sue for breach of contract, because the terms of his employment were broken. If you want another good example, look at the case of *Boyo v Lambeth Borough Council* [1994] to see how the judges viewed the precedent set in Gunton.

A further important point about wrongful dismissal is that it deals with what is a very important point for a sacked employee: compensation in the form of damages. If you're dismissed from your job, you don't necessarily want to get your job back, but you do want to be compensated for the loss of salary and also for all the other problems associated with suddenly becoming unemployed. If you remember, in contract law, damages are paid to restore the parties to the original position they were in before the contract was breached. This can cover wages or salary which should have been paid during the notice period, and holiday pay and loss of pension, as well as other perks, such as a company car. Employees can also claim interest on the whole amount from the time they lost their job to the court hearing.

So what exactly have we looked at this morning? Well, to sum up, we need to understand that the major difference between unfair dismissal and wrongful dismissal is that unfair dismissal is an invention of statutory law whereas wrongful dismissal follows the common law rules. Well, how does this actually affect the people who have lost their jobs? They might think of this as nothing more than legal semantics, but it may have an outcome on their cases in a number of different ways.

Firstly, whereas unfair dismissal can only be claimed if a person has at least one year's continuous service, there is no such restriction with wrongful dismissal. Secondly, unfair dismissal is regulated by statute and must go through a two-stage test. Stage 1: Was the dismissal for a fair reason? Stage 2: If the dismissal was fair, was the dismissal dealt with by following the correct procedures? In wrongful dismissal there must have been a breach of the contract of employment. A third major difference is that cases of unfair dismissal are heard before an employment tribunal whereas cases of wrongful dismissal are normally heard in the ordinary courts.

So it should be clear that these three major differences have very practical applications for the people who have lost their jobs. They're not just esoteric concepts that we lawyers love to debate.

I strongly recommend that you study the case of *Wise Group* v *Mitchell* [2005] All ER 168. It clearly sets out the differences between unfair and wrongful dismissal …

Unit 9, Lesson 2, Exercise D 🎧 2.3

1 Increasingly we find that when people do lose their jobs, especially when they believe it's through no fault of their own, they want to know how the law will protect them.

2 Now, in terms of the contract of employment, the employer must have a good reason for dismissing the employee and has to show that the reason is genuine and justifies the dismissal.

3 As we shall see, the courts take a different approach when employees have lost their jobs after being with a company for less than a year.

4 It could be argued that the management simply believed that the employee was incompetent and unable to carry out the task, regardless of whether or not training was offered.

5 From the point of view of the contract, a serious breach would be something like a complete change of the job description or a substantial reduction in pay.

6 Of course, it's true to say that the same reason can also be given in cases of unfair dismissal because your employer has a genuine reason which justifies your dismissal.

7 Research has shown that in fact the courts did frequently find in favour of the employer.

8 So it should be clear that these three major differences have very practical applications for the people who have lost their jobs.

Unit 9, Lesson 3, Exercise A 🎧 2.4

1 'wrongful, 'statute, re'solve, 'conduct

2 pro'vision, tri'bunal, dis'missal, 'damages

3 em'ployment law, 'common law, breach of 'contract, re'tirement age

4 'actually, 'generally, 'usually, de'monstrably, 'crucially

Unit 9, Lesson 3, Exercise C 🎧 2.5

Part 3

OK, so moving on to look at some of the statutes involving unfair dismissal. The key statute is the Employment Rights Act 1996, where what constitutes *fair* dismissal is defined. If you look at section 98 of the ERA you will see that the reasons for fair dismissal are covered under six heads. I'm going to go through the six heads quickly, then look in more detail at two of them.

Number one is conduct. That is, the way in which you behave at work. If, for example, you frequently come to work under the influence of drugs or alcohol, your employer has a legitimate reason to dismiss you. Number two is capability. Employees should have the necessary skills and qualifications to do the job to the required standard. If they do not, there are grounds for fair dismissal. Thirdly, there is redundancy. If the company closes down or downsizes, there may be no more work for the employee to do. The next head is retirement. If an employee reaches the normal retirement age, or 65 if there is no normal retirement age, the employer has the right to dismiss, provided the correct procedures have been followed. We then have what is known as 'statutory restriction'. This is where an employee is no longer able to perform the job, because, in doing so, they would be breaking the law. An example of this would be if a delivery driver lost his driving licence.

Finally, there is what the ERA terms 'another substantial reason'. In other words, there is an overwhelming reason to dismiss an employee. For example, if an employee is sent to prison, or less drastically, where an employee just cannot work with a colleague because of a personality clash. Benny, Sargeant and Jefferson point out in *Employment Law,* in the *Blackstone's Law Questions and Answers* series, one of your core texts – this edition was published in 2007 – that this particular clause is open to wide interpretation. But you don't need to worry about that at this stage.

By the way, I see that some of you are using the Cornell note-taking system. That's very good. Do you all know about this? No? Right, well, if you want to know more about it, I suggest you look at *How to Study in College* by Walter Pauk, the 9th edition, published in 2007. It's very good, and it should be in the university library. I'm sure that you all know the importance of taking good notes – and this system is particularly useful.

So to get back to the main topic. I said we would look in more detail at two of the heads – they are, on the slide, the third and the fourth, redundancy and retirement. Redundancy first. This is a complex area in employment law. One definition of redundancy given by *thefreedictionary.com* on the Web is: 'the state or fact of being unemployed because work is no longer offered or considered necessary.' Typically, this means that someone's job disappears and this can happen for a number of different reasons; not just advances in technology, which make some types of job obsolete.

Now the fourth head under which an employee can be fairly dismissed is retirement. Of course this is different from redundancy, because it depends on the employee's age. To be more precise, retirement occurs when someone reaches what is known as normal retirement age. This is usually specified in the contract of employment. If it isn't specified, courts will now construe this as 65 for both men and women. In the past, of course, women could retire at 60. The change came into force on 1st October 2006 under the Employment Equality (Age) Regulations. So to summarize, briefly, this particular part of employment law: 'redundancy' is a precise legal term. If an employer feels that an employee isn't pulling his weight, the employer can't just say there is no longer a job for the employee to do. The same is true of retirement. An employer can dismiss an employee at his contractual age of retirement. They can't sack him, under this head, as a cover for unfair dismissal, just because they think he's getting on a bit and isn't performing as well as they would like.

OK, so now we've seen on what grounds an employer can dismiss an employee fairly. And under these heads, what rights an employee might have to claim unfair dismissal. To quote Benny, Sargeant and Jefferson, 'The basis of UD is statutory. Therefore it is governed by statute. In a case where the dismissal is not automatically unfair the employee must prove that he or she is qualified and has been dismissed. The burden of proof then switches to the employers to show that they had one of five possible potentially fair reasons: capability, conduct, redundancy, statutory illegality and some other substantial reason.'

Now I think that's all I'm going to say for the moment on the basic parts of unfair dismissal. Are there any questions so far? … No, good. Now when I see you in tutorials, we'll look in more detail at the case law in wrongful dismissal. In the meantime, I'm going to set you a research task. Right, now listen carefully … your task is to find out about the different cases that have created

precedents to develop the common law approach to wrongful, as opposed to unfair, dismissal.

Unit 9, Lesson 3, Exercise D 🎧 2.6

Extract 1

Finally, there is what the ERA terms 'another substantial reason'. In other words, there is an overwhelming reason to dismiss an employee. For example, if an employee is sent to prison, or less drastically, where an employee just cannot work with a colleague because of a personality clash. Benny, Sargeant and Jefferson point out in *Employment Law*, in the *Blackstone's Law Questions and Answers* series, one of your core texts – this edition was published in 2007 – that this particular clause is open to wide interpretation.

Extract 2

By the way, I see that some of you are using the Cornell note-taking system. That's very good. Do you all know about this? No? Right, well, if you want to know more about it, I suggest you look at *How to Study in College* by Walter Pauk, the 9th edition, published in 2007. It's very good, and it should be in the university library.

Extract 3

So to get back to the main topic. I said we would look in more detail at two of the heads – they are, on the slide, the third and the fourth, redundancy and retirement. Redundancy first. This is a complex area in employment law. One definition of redundancy given by *thefreedictionary.com* on the Web is: 'the state or fact of being unemployed because work is no longer offered or considered necessary.' Typically, this means that someone's job disappears and this can happen for a number of different reasons; not just advances in technology, which make some types of job obsolete.

Extract 4

OK, so now we've seen on what grounds an employer can dismiss an employee fairly. And under these heads, what rights an employee might have to claim unfair dismissal. To quote Benny, Sargeant and Jefferson, 'The basis of UD is statutory. Therefore it is governed by statute. In a case where the dismissal is not automatically unfair, the employee must prove that he or she is qualified and has been dismissed. The burden of proof then switches to the employers to show that they had one of five possible potentially fair reasons: capability, conduct, redundancy, statutory illegality and some other substantial reason.'

Unit 9, Lesson 4, Exercise D 🎧 2.7

Extract 1

… Claiming unfair dismissal is the usual way a sacked employee will seek redress against an employer. The rules for claiming unfair dismissal are relatively straightforward as they're laid down in various statutory provisions. However, there are a number of disadvantages. Firstly, you have to have at least one year's continuous service with the same company in order to be able to claim unfair dismissal. It seems that sometimes employers take advantage of this and sack employees after they have worked for 11 months. Secondly, there is a cap on the amount of compensation you can claim in an employment tribunal. Thirdly, if you don't belong to a union, you may need to employ an expensive barrister to present your case …

Extract 2

… erm, I think one big difference is wrongful dismissal. This is very important. It's possible … we can see, how this is very important. So let's look at the case of Sweet and … oh, sorry, that's the wrong case, just a minute … right, so here are some differences between unfair and wrongful … er … you can see, I think, this difference… do you have any questions about this case? …

Extract 3

… Sometimes it is a good idea in cases of unfair or wrongful dismissal to employ a barrister. Usually, this is very expensive, but it is necessary, because a barrister will present your case in the best possible way. Also, a good barrister is important because under English law you have to make sure that the rights of both the employer and the employee are fully protected …

Extract 4

… Under section 98 of the Employment Rights Act 1996, there are six reasons under which an employee can be fairly dismissed. First of all there is conduct, or the way the employee behaves at work. Secondly, capability, which means the skills and qualifications the employee needs to carry out the job to the required standard. Thirdly, redundancy, where a company or organization closes down, for example, or where there is no longer any work for the employee to do. Retirement is the next reason – where the employee reaches the normal retirement age. Then we have statutory restriction, where an employee would be breaking the law by continuing to perform the job. The final category is called 'another substantial reason'. This has been defined as an overwhelming reason to dismiss an employee. An example might be where the employee has been given a prison sentence.

Unit 11, Lesson 2, Exercise B 🎧 2.8

Part 1

Good morning. My name is Dr Sara Smith and I'm a legal consultant. It's a pleasure to be here today. I'm going to try and explain some of the external pressures on national legal systems, that is to say, I shall mainly be looking at international law and the way in which it can affect a country's domestic laws.

External pressures come mainly from international law, and there are two main categories of international law – public and private. We will look at each one in turn to see its impact on domestic law. Finally, I'm going to talk a little about polygamy – that is, multiple marriages by one person at the same time, as an example of private international law in action.

Don't misunderstand me, I don't want to imply that these external pressures totally determine the way a country's internal legal system operates. I wouldn't go as far as Lord Denning, who, when talking about the influence of the European Union on the United Kingdom, said that European Union law is 'like a tidal wave, bringing down our sea walls and flowing inland over our fields and houses.'

International law certainly doesn't *govern* domestic law, in *any* country, but we will see that it has become much more important over the last one hundred years.

It is fair to say that, nowadays, domestic courts in most countries keep an eye on decisions that are made at an international level. However, to some degree, the same laws will be interpreted differently in different countries. International law exerts an influence on domestic law, then, and, not only that, but it also influences internal government policies at the same time.

Unit 11, Lesson 2, Exercise C 🎧 2.9

Part 2

Let's look first at what is generally known as public international law. Public international law concerns the relationship between sovereign nations. It has developed mainly through international conventions, though custom can play an important role. Its modern development began in the middle of the 19th century. The two world wars, the League of Nations and other international organizations such as the International Labour Organization or ILO helped to establish many of the foundations of modern public international law. After the Second World War, the League of Nations was replaced by the United Nations, founded under the UN Charter. One of the principal pillars of this is the Universal Declaration of Human Rights. Other international norms and laws have been established through international agreements such as the Geneva Conventions on the conduct of armed conflicts. All these have had both a direct and indirect influence on a country's sovereignty. However, recent international conflicts provide a good example of how individual countries interpret the role of the UN and the ways in which the Geneva Conventions should operate.

Increasingly, in the modern world, public international law, as reflected in international conventions and agreements, is influenced, directly or indirectly, by pressure groups. There is Greenpeace, for instance, who campaign on environmental issues. Their work to save whales has certainly influenced countries in their attitude to the worldwide ban on whaling. Another environmental organization is Friends of the Earth, which, as well as campaigning for the environment, also tries to control the immense power of big businesses, such as Tesco, the largest UK supermarket chain. Their work has led to changes in food laws in some countries.

An important aspect of the international law landscape is, of course, the regional trade organizations – such as the EU or Mercosur, or ASEAN – which governments may elect to belong to. These groups provide a highly advantageous internal market and often protect their members from competition from businesses from outside the group. But these trade organizations then determine, to a large extent, who a particular country is allowed to trade with. There are quotas for goods from countries outside the trading group, for example, which members of the group must stick to. A good example of this is the situation in 2005 involving the flood of Chinese textile imports into the EU. Too many Chinese clothing products came into Europe, breaching the quota limits allowed. European manufacturers were afraid that European jobs would suffer and the clothes were kept locked in warehouses until an agreement was reached. This may seem like a matter of economics, not law, but of course the quota system and the action taken when quotas are exceeded come from the international trade agreement in the first place.

There are also other organizations, such as the World Bank or the World Trade Organization, which can have a strong influence on how countries run their economies. The World Bank will often tell a country exactly how to behave economically if it wants to borrow money from the organization. The WTO deals with the rules of trade between nations. The main structure of the WTO is a set of trading agreements, which are negotiated and then signed up to by the governments of the world's trading nations. Again, is this about economics or law? It's about both. To the extent that disputes between states fall outside a unified legal framework, this raises issues of the enforceability of standard practices.

Of course, the burning issue of the moment is climate change. To what extent can public international law have a major influence in this area? Some people say that international agreements have done nothing to change the actual behaviour of some nation states. The evidence shows that this is especially true with respect to the United States. In my view, the refusal of the US to sign up to the Kyoto Protocol is a case in point. This failure set a very bad role model. A very good article by Jana von Stein called *The International Law and Politics of Climate Change* has some interesting ideas on how the creators of international environment agreements can design mechanisms that deter defection without deterring participation. In other words, how the lawmakers can create international agreements which people actually sign up to, rather than run away from because their conditions are too harsh. Briefly, in her paper, von Stein argues that the harder a treaty is, the more 'selective' states are about ratification. She has no doubt that harder treaties may actually deter states from joining, and I quote: 'these institutional features may deter from joining the very states whose environmental practices are least consistent with the treaty's requirements.'

So, as we can see, the effect of public international law on domestic law is very important, particularly in the context of today's multinational and global environment.

Now, let's turn to another aspect of international law: 'conflict of laws', as it is mainly known under common law jurisdictions, or 'private international law'. Unlike public international law, it deals with conflicts involving private persons rather than states or other important international bodies. The plaintiff in a case usually petitions for where the case should be heard. The court then decides whether, in fact, it has the jurisdiction to hear the case. If it has, it will then decide what characterization of law, such as family law, tort or contract, the case should be heard under.

Let's take as an example an area of family law: the question of polygamous marriage. In many countries, it is legal under strict conditions to marry more than one person. If the family then moves to another country where polygamous marriage is illegal, then what is the legal position of the family in the event of a dispute? The Private International Law (Miscellaneous Provisions) Act 1995 states in part II section 5, validity in English law of potentially polygamous marriages, that: 'A marriage entered into outside England and Wales between parties neither of whom is already married is not void under the law of England and Wales on the ground that it is entered into under a law which permits polygamy and that either party is domiciled in England and Wales.' So English law still does not allow bigamy. It simply accepts that a first marriage in a country that allows polygamy is legal in England and Wales.

Some countries go further in their interpretation. In the legal systems of many states, polygamous marriage is recognized provided it was entered into validly and the ceremony was performed according to the law of the country in which the marriage took place. This is the so-called *lex loci* rule. However, in the United States, for example, it is illegal to enter into a polygamous marriage. Courts have also held that where people cohabit in a polygamous marriage made in a country where it is valid, this will not be recognized.

Unit 11, Lesson 2, Exercise F 🎧 2.10

Some people say that international agreements have done nothing to change the actual behaviour of some nation states. The evidence shows that this is especially true with respect to the United States. In my view, the refusal of the US to sign up to the Kyoto Protocol is a case in point. This failure set a very bad role model. A very good article by Jana von Stein called *The International Law and*

Politics of Climate Change has some interesting ideas on how the creators of international environment agreements can design mechanisms that deter defection without deterring participation. In other words, how the lawmakers can create international agreements which people actually sign up to, rather than run away from because their conditions are too harsh.

Unit 11, Lesson 2, Exercise G 🎧 2.11

1 I'm going to try and explain some of the external pressures on national legal systems, that is to say, I shall mainly be looking at international law and the way in which it can affect a country's domestic laws.

2 Don't misunderstand me, I don't want to imply that these external pressures totally determine the way a country's internal legal system operates.

3 I wouldn't go as far as Lord Denning, who, when talking about the influence of the European Union on the United Kingdom, said that European Union law is 'like a tidal wave, bringing down our sea walls and flowing inland over our fields and houses.'

4 It is fair to say that, nowadays, domestic courts in most countries keep an eye on decisions that are made at an international level.

5 However, to some degree, the same laws will be interpreted differently in different countries.

6 International law exerts an influence on domestic law, then, and, not only that, but it also influences internal government policies at the same time.

7 To the extent that disputes between states fall outside a unified legal framework, this raises issues of the enforceability of standard practices.

8 The evidence shows that this is especially true with respect to the United States.

9 In my view, the refusal of the US to sign up to the Kyoto Protocol is a case in point.

10 A very good article by Jana von Stein called *The International Law and Politics of Climate Change* has some interesting ideas on how the creators of international environment agreements can design mechanisms that deter defection without deterring participation.

11 Briefly, in her paper, von Stein argues that the harder a treaty is, the more 'selective' states are about ratification.

12 She has no doubt that harder treaties may actually deter states from joining, and I quote: 'these institutional features may deter from joining the very states whose environmental practices are least consistent with the treaty's requirements.'

Unit 11, Lesson 3, Exercise A 🎧 2.12

a,lleged 'criminal

,crimes against hu'manity

do,mestic 'law

extra'dition ,crimes

,fugitive from 'justice

i,mmunity from prose'cution

inter,national con'vention

ju,dicial au'thorities

'sovereign i,mmunity

uni,versal juris'diction

Unit 11, Lesson 3, Exercise B 🎧 2.13

Part 3

I want now to draw your attention to another aspect of public international law which has an impact on domestic law, and that is extradition. As I am sure you are aware, extradition is the return of an alleged criminal or fugitive from justice to the country in which the alleged offence occurred. We can say, for example, that a person accused of committing a crime in Spain was extradited from the United Kingdom – to Spain, of course. The key question is: in what circumstances can a person be extradited? Some people claim that extradition should only apply to serious crimes, others say that certain people, such as heads of state, should be exempt from extradition. I agree with the first but I just cannot accept the second. Perhaps the most controversial aspect of extradition is the concept of universal jurisdiction. Crimes against humanity, such as torture and genocide, the systematic destruction of a religious or ethnic group, have a special place in international law. These offences may be punished by *any* state on the grounds that, as the trial judge stated in *Demjanjuk* v *Petrovsky* [1985].'The offenders are common enemies of mankind and all nations have an equal interest in their apprehension and prosecution.'

So, in normal extradition, a person commits a crime in country X and flees to country Y. The government of country X asks the government of country Y to send him back, or extradite him. But, in the case of crimes against humanity, country Z can ask country Y to extradite the person. Why? The most common reason is that the person has harmed, in some way, citizens of country Z in country X. Is that clear? I think I got it right!

Let's consider the well-known but very complex case involving General Augusto Pinochet, the former President of Chile. He became the President of Chile in 1973 and, after he came to power, was alleged to have been indirectly responsible for the murder or disappearance of a large number of his political opponents, including Spanish citizens. The evidence against the general was compelling. Indeed, as one of the Law Lords pointed out, the facts of the case were not in dispute. In 1998, Pinochet came to London for medical treatment. The Spanish judicial authorities wanted to extradite Pinochet to Spain for these alleged human rights abuses, even though they were committed mainly in Chile and not in Spain. The argument was that the crimes Pinochet had committed were international crimes that were covered by convention and, for these crimes, a person did not have to be extradited to the country where the alleged abuses were committed. The British government put Pinochet under house arrest, pending the outcome of the extradition plea.

Lawyers for the general claimed that he had sovereign immunity because he had been the head of state at the time the alleged abuses occurred. Under common law, a head of state is entitled to immunity from prosecution for actions that were carried out in an official capacity. It is quite clear to me that this argument is false, and the House of Lords agrees with me. They found, by a 3-to-2 majority, that torture was a crime against international law and, for this particular crime, Pinochet was not entitled to immunity and therefore could be extradited to Spain. As it happens, in this case, no extradition took place. Pinochet was deemed too ill to answer the charges and was released by the British government to return to Chile, where he died in 2006.

Clearly, this idea of universal jurisdiction is controversial in international law. The arguments for it are that certain crimes pose such a threat to the international community that there should be no safe haven for anyone who has committed these so-called acts against humanity. However, some people claim that universal jurisdiction is a breach of an individual state's sovereignty. Under

the United Nations Charter, all states are equal in sovereignty.

The request for the extradition of a head of state is a very unusual one, occasionally involving a few countries. But now, I'm going to set you a task connected with international public law which potentially involves *all* the countries in the world. Perhaps you can guess what the topic is – global warming. I want you to do some research into what steps the international community has already taken to counter the effects of climate change. I want you to focus, firstly, on the different international agreements that have addressed environmental problems, particularly with respect to the effects of global warming. Secondly, I'd like you to think about whether these measures to protect the environment could actually be realistically enforced under international law. Finally, I want you to research the precautionary principle. What is it? What is its effect on international law in the area of climate change legislation?

Unit 11, Lesson 3, Exercise E 2.14

The key question is: in what circumstances can a person be extradited? Some people claim that extradition should only apply to serious crimes, others say that certain people, such as heads of state, should be exempt from extradition. I agree with the first but I just cannot accept the second. In the Pinochet case, lawyers for the general claimed that he had sovereign immunity because he had been the head of state at the time the alleged abuses occurred. It is quite clear to me that this argument is false. There was no doubt of his guilt – the evidence against the general was compelling. Indeed, as one of the Law Lords pointed out, these facts were not in dispute.

Unit 11, Lesson 4, Exercise B 2.15

Rio Declaration

Kyoto Protocol

human rights

League of Nations

Friends of the Earth

Geneva Conventions

Emissions Trading Scheme

European Union

Intergovernmental Panel on Climate Change

Unit 11, Lesson 4, Exercise E 2.16

Extract 1

The lecturer asked us to research the precautionary principle, particularly in relation to climate change legislation. In my part of the seminar, I would like to define the principle then explain its relevance to environmental laws. Some people say that the climate is changing but many scientists argue that there is no actual proof of this. The precautionary principle states that we must do something to protect ourselves and our children from damage, even if the scientific evidence is not complete. The environmental pressure group Greenpeace, for one, believes in the precautionary principle, pointing out that we have nothing to lose and everything to gain from acting now.

Extract 2

OK, following on from what Majed has said, I'd like to mention some important environmental initiatives. The year 1992 paved the way for the convergence of the precautionary principle, climate change and international law. At Rio de Janeiro, the world acknowledged the precautionary principle in international law when it adopted the United Nations Framework on Climate Change or UNFCC. It basically said that a lack of full scientific research should not stop people from taking action to mitigate the effects of climate change.

Extract 3

Right. Thank you, Evie. I'm going to expand the topic by mentioning the counter argument. The precautionary principle sounds great in theory. I'm sure everyone agrees that we should carefully weigh up the risks and benefits of our actions. However, in my view, it cannot be a good way of evaluating evidence to give more weight to things that have not been scientifically proven. I remember reading somewhere that if we had applied the precautionary principle to the effects of fire, we would all have ended up eating our food raw. And what about other scientific advances such as the development of the X-ray? If the precautionary principle had been implemented, it would probably never have been used in hospitals. In relation to climate change, the precautionary principle says: Act now just in case. In legal terms, the precautionary principle changes the burden of proof. It says to scientists: We will act unless you can prove something is *not* harmful. It's like saying: We will convict this man unless you can prove he didn't kill his wife. The burden of proof in most legal systems is the other way round.

We will not convict this man unless you can prove he *did* kill his wife. It is impossible to prove a negative, as all scientists know, so the precautionary principle is bad science and bad law.

Extract 4

As well as environmental issues we can also look at another area in which the precautionary principle can be put into practice. Here, I'm going to explain how countries have often used it to justify their interventionist policies. If you think there is a risk posed by another country, you can take action on the grounds that it's better to be safe than sorry. This may result in large numbers of civilian casualties but these can be justified because you claim that the consequences of not intervening are likely to be far more serious. This is, of course, pure speculation and under these circumstances can never be proved. It is impossible to know what these dire consequences of non-intervention would be, as the country has already intervened! I think this is the same situation with global warming. People use the most extreme forecasts about the terrible effects of global warming and use those to justify the actions that need to be taken because *not* to take them would pose an even greater risk. I would argue that taking steps to limit global warming actually has a major effect on the economic growth of countries that can least afford it and could result in the loss of just as many lives as in a war against terrorism, if you can ever have a war against terrorism.